Managing the Sea's Living Resources

Lexington Books Studies in Marine Affairs
John King Gamble, Jr., Editor

William R. Rosengren, Michael S. Bassis, *The Social Organization of Nautical Education*

Mark W. Janis, *Sea Power and the Law of the Sea*

Louis E. Cellineri, *Seaport Dynamics*

Robert B. Ditton, John L. Seymour, Gerald C. Swanson, *Coastal Resources Management*

John King Gamble, Jr., *Marine Policy*

H. Gary Knight, *Managing the Sea's Living Resources*

Managing the Sea's Living Resources

**Legal and Political Aspects
of High Seas Fisheries**

H. Gary Knight
Louisiana State University Law Center

Studies in Marine Affairs

Lexington Books
D.C. Heath and Company
Lexington, Massachusetts
Toronto

Library of Congress Cataloging in Publication Data

Knight, Herbert Gary, 1939-
    Managing the sea's living resources.

    Bibliography: p.
    Includes index.
    1. Fishery management, International. 2. Fishery law and legis-
lation— United States. I. Title.
SH328.K59   333.9'5   76-20042
ISBN 0-669-00874-5

Copyright © 1977 by D.C. Heath and Company

All rights reserved. No part of this publication may be reproduced or transmitted in any form or by any means, electronic or mechanical, including
photocopy, recording, or any information storage or retrieval system,
without permission in writing from the publisher.

Published simultaneously in Canada.

Printed in the United States of America.

International Standard Book Number: 0-669-00874-5

Library of Congress Catalog Card Number: 76-20042

To
Becky,
who loves to fish

Contents

List of Figures and Tables

Preface

This book was commissioned at a critical point in the history of international fisheries management and law of the sea. The old regime is collapsing while the new regime is as yet discernable only in its bare outlines. I think it is appropriate, then, that this work be undertaken to pose some of the problems of international fisheries management, to summarize the history of the legal and political aspects of the attempt to manage high seas fisheries, and to describe the new jurisdictional arrangements from which future management will likely emanate.

Although the Third United Nations Conference on the Law of the Sea has not as of this writing reached a definitive agreement adopting treaty articles concerning the management of the living resources of the sea, the trend of international thinking is obvious, and it is being manifested daily in new national claims to exclusive fisheries management over 200-mile zones. The most complex of those unilateral claims is that asserted by the United States in its "Fishery Conservation and Management Act of 1976" (FCMA). I have devoted a fairly long chapter to an explanation of the FCMA. I have done this for several reasons. First, it is the most complex and well thought out of all the fishery management systems included in 200-mile jurisdictional claims. Second, it is designed not to be simply an exercise in chauvinism but to provide a mechanism for the rational management of fisheries; it may therefore provide a model that other nations will follow, albeit carefully noting its successes and its failures. Third, it is the most articulate of such claims, thereby giving us the most detailed view of a very possible future—the new regime for international fisheries management.

The FCMA is not a perfect piece of legislation and is apt to undergo amendment at an early stage. Further, the regulations promulgated pursuant to the statute and the day-to-day operation of developing, implementing, and enforcing fishery management plans adopted pursuant to the FCMA are as yet ill-defined. Nonetheless, in my opinion there is no better indication of the future than the FCMA, and it is for that reason that I have concentrated on it in this book as an indication of the type of jurisdictional fishery pattern that we may expect to see in the future.

Baton Rouge, Louisiana   *H.G.K.*
October 31, 1976

Acknowledgments

I am indebted to a large number of people for my knowledge of international fishery management problems and for their direct and indirect contributions to this book. In particular I should like to thank John King Gamble who recommended me to Lexington Books for the purpose of preparing this volume. Also, special notes of thanks go to John Lawrence Hargrove, Director of Studies at the American Society of International Law and Robert E. Stein, now with the International Institute for Environment and Development, both of whom made possible substantial amounts of research and publication of results under auspices of the American Society of International Law.

Sincere appreciation is also conveyed to Paul M. Hebert, Dean, Louisiana State University Law Center, who has provided an environment that has greatly facilitated my academic and research activities particularly with respect to his effort in establishing the Campanile Professorship of Marine Resources Law to which I was appointed in 1971 and which has been the primary source of research funds for my work in law of the sea. I am also indebted to the Office of Sea Grant Programs (National Oceanic and Atmospheric Administration, Department of Commerce) that since 1968 has generously supported my research work in the field of law of the sea and, under the able administration of Dr. Jack R. Van Lopik at Louisiana State University, has permitted me a wide range of education, research, and advisory service activities. My gratitude also extends to my indefatigable secretary, Ms. Marianne Didier, who typed and proofread the entire manuscript and the annexes, and who also handled administrative matters in connection with the book.

Finally, there is a group of people who have, in ways of which they are each aware, assisted me in my research and thinking about international fisheries management issues. The list includes: John R. Botzum, President, Nautilus Press, Washington, D.C. (publisher of *Ocean Science News* and *Marine Fish Management,* both of which were of great value in analyzing current fisheries management issues); Professor William T. Burke, University of Washington School of Law; Dr. Francis T. Christy, Resources for the Future, Inc.; August J. Felando, Esq., of the California Bar; Eugene R. Fidell, Esq., of the Washington, D.C. bar; Dr. Ted B. Ford, Office of Sea Grant Development, Louisiana State University; Professor Edgar Gold, Dalhousie Law School; Lieutenant Commander Michael J. Jacobs; Professor Jon L. Jacobson, University of Oregon School of Law; Professor Douglas Johnston, Dalhousie Law School; Professor Albert W. Koers, University of Utrecht, the Netherlands; William Nelson Utz, Esq., of the Washington, D.C. bar; and, James P. Walsh, Esq., Committee on Commerce, U.S. Senate.

1

Prologue I: The Law of the Sea Crisis and the Tragedy of the Commons

The Law of the Sea Crisis

No knowledgeable observer of international ocean affairs will deny that there literally exists today a crisis in the law of the sea generally and concerning high seas fisheries management in particular. As evidenced by the convening of the Third United Nations Conference on the Law of the Sea—the largest and most complex negotiation in the history of the world—as well as by the increasing number of unilateral claims to national jurisdiction over the ocean, the law of the sea is clearly in an unstable condition, and change is clearly impending. The causes of the crisis and its roots in and relation to high seas fisheries management will be identified and discussed in Chapter 3.

Any crisis can, however, when viewed in the perspective of time, be clearly understood as the turning point in people's perceptions about a particular problem. A course of action may have been followed by nations for decades or perhaps centuries without giving rise to much controversy or conflict. Then, suddenly, because of some technological innovation or political or social change, that course of action begins to produce more waste or conflict than benefits. After a period of adjustment, a new course of action develops (perhaps over a substantial period of time, through uniform national practice; perhaps in a very short time, as a result of a treaty adopted by the affected nations) and a new "routine" is followed henceforth. Such crisis points are almost always marked by violence and disruption of order, and for those involved it is often difficult to perceive the crisis as a stage in a progressive development. The immediate problem is to "win" the conflict or put out the fire, and the fact that these are simply manifestations of a change in historical direction is usually lost on those charged with handling the present emergency. So it is with international fisheries management.

Decision makers are faced today with such problems as tuna boat seizures in the South Pacific Ocean, the "cod war" in the North Atlantic, the disastrous overfishing of certain stocks of fish throughout the world, and the impact of national security issues on the resolution of fishery conflicts. In considering these "brush fires" we often fail to perceive them as simply the sparks resulting from the inevitable friction as one historical course of action conflicts with another emerging course.

This book attempts to contribute to an understanding of the past legal and political components of high seas fishery management and of the almost certain

1

future direction of that management process, with the hope that the period 1950~1980 can be better seen as an era of transition and not as a permanent state of affairs in itself.

The purposes of this book, then, are to examine the *legal and political* factors that led to the characterization of high seas fishery resources as common property; to discuss some of the conflicts which ensued as a result of that characterization; and to analyze the emerging trend away from common property rights in fishery resources.

The Tragedy of the Commons

In 1968, just as the current law of the sea negotiations were getting underway at the United Nations, biologist Garret Hardin expounded the theory of the "tragedy of the commons" in a short article in *Science*.[1] It is worth outlining that thesis here because of its relevance to the problem of international fisheries management.

Hardin postulated an open pasture or range (the "commons") on which a number of herdsmen raised cattle. Although new herdsmen could introduce new herds to the commons, and although the herdsmen already there might occasionally add more cattle to their existing herds, the system worked. That is, the common property resource—the grass—was not exhausted, because various factors such as war and disease kept the amount of grazing below the capacity of the land to sustain this "harvest." At some point in time, however, science and technology led to the eradication of those factors that kept the demand on the "commons" at a relatively low level. It became theoretically possible to keep more cattle alive and grazing than the carrying capacity of the land would sustain.

Each herdsman now engaged in a private inquiry concerning the ultimate value to him of adding one or more animals to his herd. Assuming that he were one of five herdsmen each of which ran five cattle on the commons, our hypothetical herdsman might contemplate adding one cow, calculating that the positive value of his action represents an increase in personal income to him of about 20% while the negative value would only be an additional 1/25 "strain" on the commons (Table 1-1). This sort of calculation would lead him to conclude that it was to his benefit to add one animal, then another, and then another. Our herdsman may or may not be aware of the limit or carrying capacity of the land, but he is reluctant not to add to his herd because to do so will put more food in his children's stomachs or more money in the bank, while to refrain from doing so gains him nothing and, worse, leaves him no assurance that the other four herdsmen will not take advantage of his abstinence to increase their own herds and their own incomes, partially at his expense.

The problem—the "tragedy" according to Hardin—is that each of the

Table 1-1
The Economics of the Rational Herdsman and the Commons

Net benefit to one individual herdsman:
  At Present   —   5 cattle
  Add   —   1 cow
  New Total   6 cattle
  Percent Increase =   20 percent
Net loss to one individual herdsman:
  Present cattle using commons   25
  Add   1
  New Total   26
  Percent increase in demand (strain on entire commons) =   4 percent
Net gain = +16 percent

herdsmen is thinking in a similar manner and each will thus add one animal, then another, and then another, until shortly there may be fifty animals on the commons the carrying capacity of which may be only twenty-five animals. The grazing land will then be exhausted, and ruin will fall upon all the herdsmen.

An identical scenario would follow if instead of each individual herdsman increasing his herd, new herdsmen chanced by the commons, saw that it provided good grassland, and not excluded by any laws relating to residence in the area, added their herds to the commons thus pushing the carrying capacity of the land beyond the breaking point. What is happening in both of these hypothetical situations is that the rational herdsman or new entrant is securing benefits for himself while distributing losses among the other herdsmen. In his article Hardin concluded that:

Each man is locked into a system that compels him to increase his herd without limit—in a world that is limited. Ruin is the destination toward which all men rush, each pursuing his own interests in a society that believes in the freedom of the commons. Freedom in a commons brings ruin to all.[2]

Because the tragedy of the commons is directly analogous to the problem of high seas fisheries management, one might inquire whether there are solutions to the situation described by Hardin. At least two approaches immediately recommend themselves. First, one might sell off the commons as private property with each herdsman taking a specific plot of land. In this situation the herdsman may well consider adding more cattle to his herd, seeking to maximize his own benefit, but he must now realize that losses will be distributed only to himself, not allocated among other herdsmen in the area. Thus when the carrying capacity of the land is reached, the utility of adding an additional cow still remains, but the negative impact exceeds the benefit, thus working a natural constraint on the herdsman's tendency to destroy the grazing capacity of his private property.

Second, one might keep the commons as public property but impose restrictions on it, including the right to limit and regulate access. The right to enter would be controlled by some entity (perhaps governmental) and the system of allocation could be selected from among many alternatives—on the basis of wealth, by the use of an auction system; on a merit basis, as defined by agreed standards; on the basis of a lottery; or on a first-come, first-served basis. Assuming agreement could be reached on a system of allocation, the entity entrusted with limiting access to the commons could thereby ensure that the carrying capacity of the land was not exceeded.

As will be noted in more detail in succeeding chapters, the evolution of the international law of the sea has led to the characterization of fishery resources beyond the limits of the territorial seas as common property resources. New fishermen continue to enter a fishery, and fishermen already in it continue to increase their effort, until the carrying capacity of the stock—its "sustainable yield"—is exceeded, at which point the continued effort tends to deplete the stock, ultimately reaching a point where it becomes economically disadvantageous to engage in fishing at all because of the very small size of the catch. At this point all is in ruin, for there are a great many fishermen seeking their livelihood from harvesting fish—the stock of which has been so depleted that no entrant can even meet his expenses, much less show a profit.

Do either of the solutions posed to the tragedy of the commons apply to high seas fisheries? The allocation of private property rights is a conceivable answer, though there must first, of course, be some governmental entity endowed with the authority to allocate the resource and dispose of it to private purchasers. As will be observed in more detail in Chapter 3, the evolution of the law of the sea has characterized those ocean areas beyond relatively narrow territorial water limits as not being subject to appropriation by any nation or person. So long, then, as this nonappropriation rule of international law is binding and effective, it will be impossible to create private property rights in fisheries.

Likewise, the second solution offers no panacea to the problems of overfishing, since in order to develop limitations on access enforced by some governmental entity, that entity must be endowed with jurisdiction over the particular area of the ocean or stocks of fish concerned. Again, because of the concept of freedom of the high seas, this is not the case. However, as will be noted in Chapter 4, nations may well agree among themselves to accept the regulation of their own citizens for the common good by participating in some scheme for limiting the amount of effort directed at a particular fishery. This "solution" suffers from a major defect, however, because nations not choosing to voluntarily limit themselves cannot be affected due to the rights they possess under the customary international law principle of freedom of the high seas.

It would thus appear that the solution to the potential tragedy of the commons in international fisheries management must await international legal and political developments that will permit effective governmental control over areas or stocks of fish. Only then can some system of allocating access to the fish be imposed to ensure that the carrying capacity or sustainable yield of those stocks is not exceeded.

In Chapter 5 the current attempts—by international agreement and through international adjudication—to restructure the law of the sea in order to permit rational management of fisheries will be analyzed. In Chapter 6 the "unilateral" approach of claiming extended (usually 200 miles) exclusive fishing zones will be considered, with emphasis on the recently adopted United States' "Fishery Conservation and Management Act of 1976."

To set the stage for discussions of legal and political issues, however, it is first necessary to undertake a brief digression on the subjects of fishery biology and economics.

Notes

1. Garrett Hardin, "The Tragedy of the Commons," *Science,* 162 (December 1968): 1243–1248.

2. Ibid., p. 1244.

2

Prologue II: Some Elementary Fisheries Biology and Economics

In order to appreciate the impact of legal and political developments in the management of high seas fishery resources, it is necessary to have an elementary understanding of the biology and economics of fisheries. The material in this chapter is intended to provide the requisite minimum background in these areas for a better understanding of the remainder of the work.

Biology

Population Dymanics[1]

The dynamics of fish populations are such that the growth pattern indicated in Figure 2-1 is typical of a hypothetical, isolated, emerging stock of fish. From

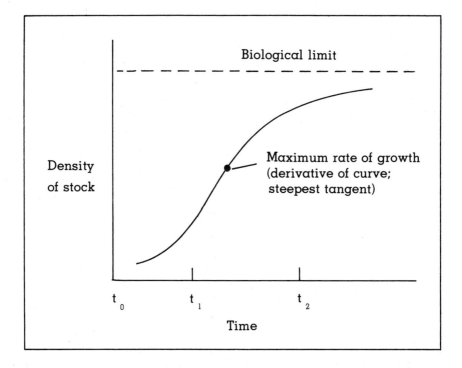

Figure 2-1. Typical Growth Pattern of a Hypothetical, Isolated, Emerging Stock of Fish.

t_0 to t_1 the population increases slowly because of the small numbers of fish available for reproduction, but from t_1 to t_2 there is a period of rapid growth occasioned by the presence of more fish of breeding age and the lack of pressure on food supplies. This is the period of maximum recruitment to the stock. After t_2 the growth rate slows because of pressure on food supplies. If one plots the rate of change of population density (dP/dt) against the population, a curve somewhat like that shown in Figure 2-2 emerges. This curve indicates that a constant harvest at the level h_0 will produce the maximum sustainable yield. Such a harvest occurs at the point of maximum recruitment to the stock and is designed, in order to maximize catch, to be equal to that recruitment. This somewhat simplified explanation is complicated in the real world by many factors. For example, harvesting must take into consideration the year-class of fish being caught to the end that younger fishes are allowed to escape while those of a prime age and weight are caught. Another complicating factor is the relationship between different stocks of fish occupying the same waters and the effects of such relationships on catch procedures. Finally, it should be noted that where fishery stocks reach maturity and spawn *annually,* an absolute maximum harvest effort may normally be permitted without adverse biologic effect, provided there is sufficient escapement to ensure a subsequent stock size commensurate with the one being fished. Such complications notwithstanding, the idea of establishing harvest in relation to maximum recruitment to a stock was the genesis of the earliest concept of fisheries management, that of "maximum sustainable yield," or MSY.

MSY has as its objective limiting catch to the largest tonnage of fish that can be taken on an indefinitely recurring basis from a given stock of fish. Environmental and other factors affecting stock size may require modifications from time to time in this sustainable yield. Fishing beyond the maximum sustainable yield will deplete the stock and will eventually result in reducing the size of the stock to the point where it becomes economically infeasible for a fishery to continue. Although it would be impossible to literally render extinct most species by overfishing, stocks can be reduced to such levels that it takes many years for them to return to size sufficient to restore an earlier sustained level of catch.

Classification Based on Migratory Habits

There are many ways to classify fish, and quite detailed scientific nomenclatures have been developed for this purpose. From the standpoint of the legal and political aspects of high seas fisheries management, however, the most significant feature of a stock of fish is its migratory pattern. These patterns become extremely important in devising suitable legal arrangements—i.e., in determining what nation or nations shall have management authority and under what

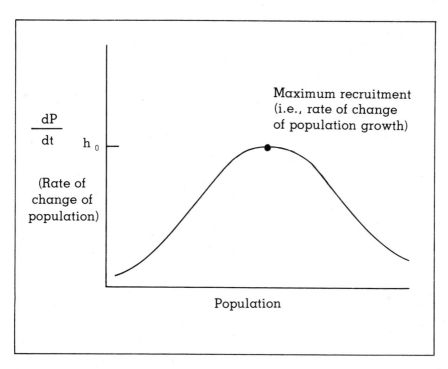

Figure 2-2. Rate of Change of Growth of a Fish Stock as a Function of Population Size.

conditions—to govern the exploitation of living marine resources. Such resources may therefore be classified in four groups—coastal, sedentary, anadromous, and highly migratory.

Coastal species are nonsedentary, free-swimming fish whose migratory patterns cause them to remain in relatively shallow continental shelf waters during their entire life cycle. Such species are almost always found within 200 miles of the coastline. They may migrate only within the coastal waters of a single nation (for example, menhaden off the Atlantic and Gulf coasts of the United States) or they may migrate through coastal waters of two or more nations (e.g., cod in the North Sea). Coastal species that migrate through the coastal waters of two or more states can be mismanaged unless all the states concerned coordinate their management systems with respect to the particular stock.

Sedentary species are those that, at the harvestable stage, either are immobile on or under the seabed or are unable to move except in physical contact with the seabed or subsoil.[2] Species of living marine resources such as oysters, clams, and crabs are universally regarded as falling within this classification.

Because of their immobility, jurisdiction over sedentary species has already been accorded exclusively to the coastal state through the Convention on the Continental Shelf.[3] Other living marine resources, such as lobsters, have behavioral patterns that have made them the object of dispute as to whether they are in fact sedentary species under the definition given in the Convention on the Continental Shelf. Current state practice is, however, toward inclusion of lobsters as a sedentary species.[4]

Anadromous species are those that breed and spend their early lives in fresh water but spend their adult lives in the open ocean ranging well beyond 200 miles from their state of origin.[5] Anadromous species ultimately return to their stream of origin to spawn, and host states often spend substantial sums of money in maintaining water quality and providing access for the returning fish.

Highly migratory species are those, such as tuna and most marine mammals, that range widely over the world ocean, not remaining for extended periods of time within any single nation's coastal waters.[6]

Economics[7]

Beginning with an article written in 1954 by H. Scott Gordon,[8] economists began examining the high seas fishery because it constituted a classic case of a "common property resource." Figure 2-3 indicates in simplified form the relation between economic effort and the conservation objectives of fisheries management. In an open access fishery, the existence of potential profit (revenue curve above cost curve) results in the addition of new fishing effort until point E_3, and perhaps even beyond. This is to be contrasted to the amount of effort, E_2, necessary to harvest MSY, and the amount of effort, E_1, necessary to produce the maximum net economic return, or profit (largest margin of revenues over costs).

If regulation is applied solely on a conservation basis, effort should be limited to E_2, with a view toward providing a renewable yield by avoiding overfishing and consequent stock depletion. If regulation is extended to economic objectives—and those objectives include optimization of economic return—then effort should be limited still further, perhaps to E_1, where net economic return would be maximized. It has been demonstrated that the effort required to produce maximum net economic return (E_1) is always less than that required to produce maximum sustainable yield (E_2).[9]

Restricting entry into a fishery in a high seas setting is very difficult, however, for under the principle of freedom of the high seas, the only method for reducing effort is voluntary agreement among nations, a device not always easy to implement. It should be obvious, however, that to achieve either maximum sustainable yield or maximum rent as an objective of international fisheries management, some restrictions or regulations must be imposed on high seas

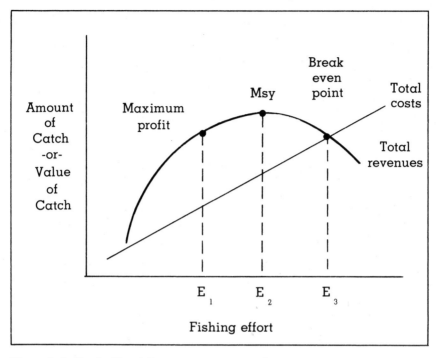

Figure 2-3. Profit (Rent) Determination in an Open Access High Seas Fishery.

fisheries. The effort to achieve such restrictions and regulations is the subject of the remainder of this book.

Notes

1. This subsection is based on material originally published by the author as "International Fisheries Management," in the L.S.U. Marine Science Teaching Aid series (rev. ed., October 1976). It is reproduced here, in revised form, with permission of the L.S.U. Center for Wetland Resources.

2. Convention on the Continental Shelf, Apr. 29, 1958, 15 U.S.T. 471 (1964), T.I.A.S. No. 5578, 499 U.N.T.S. 311 (in force, 10 June 1964), Art. 2(4).

3. Ibid., Art. 2(1).

4. See, E.G., *Offshore Shrimp Fisheries Act of 1973,* P.L. 93-242, 87 Stat. 1061, in which the lobster (*Homarus americanus*) is specified as a "continental shelf fishery resource."

5. Management of the Living Resources of the Sea: Working Paper Submitted by the Delegation of Canada, UN Doc. A/AC.138/SC.II/L.8 (27 July 1972), p. 3; Special Considerations Regarding the Management of Anadromous Fisheries and Highly Migratory Oceanic Fishes: Working Paper Submitted by the United States of America, UN Doc. A/AC.138/SC.II/L.20 (1973), p. 2.

6. Management of the Living Resources of the Sea, ibid., Special Considerations, ibid., pp. 5–10.

7. This section is based on material originally published by the author as "International Fisheries Management," in the L.S.U. Marine Science Teaching Aid series (rev. ed., October 1976). It is reproduced here, in revised form, with permission of the L.S.U. Center for Wetland Resources.

8. H. Scott Gordon, "The Economic Theory of a Common-Property Resource: The Fishery," *Journal of Political Economy* 62(1954): 124–142. See also Francis T. Christy and Anthony Scott, *The Common Wealth in Ocean Fisheries* (Baltimore, Md.: Johns Hopkins Press, 1965) and James A. Crutchfield, "Economic and Political Objectives in Fishery Management," *Transactions of the American Fisheries Society* 102(1973): 481–491.

9. Milner B. Schaefer, "Biological and Economic Aspects of the Management of Marine Fisheries," *Transactions of the American Fisheries Society* 88(1959): 100–104.

3

The History of the Law of the Sea and Its Impact on High Seas Fisheries Management

Early Developments

Although historic and prehistoric evidence indicates that from a very early date people used the sea both as a source of food and as a medium of transportation, there is very little evidence to indicate that any international concepts of law of the sea, such as we know them today, evolved prior to the Middle Ages.

Ancient Greece and Rome considered that domination of limited sea areas was possible and desirable, but there existed neither a system of international law (because the modern nation-state had yet to evolve) nor any concept of maritime freedom for persons or communities other than the controlling entity.[1] The legal status of the sea and its resources was dealt with by several Roman jurists and mention was made in at least one treatise that the sea was "common to all men."[2] Evidence indicates, however, that Rome regarded its adjacent waters and, at the height of its empire, the entire Mediterranean Sea, as a Roman lake. The concept of such waters being common to all was simply another way of expressing the right of all *Roman citizens* to the free use of the area. The concept had no international flavor because the waters dealt with by these juridical prouncements were under the exclusive control of Rome. It is doubtful whether that freedom would have been extended to other than Roman citizens had a challenge been made. In short, although the Romans recognized the utility of a freedom of the seas doctrine for internal purposes, the seas with which they dealt were in reality *mare clausum*, closed seas, totally under the domination of the Roman state.[3]

With the breakdown of social order that followed the deterioration of Roman authority, there was no single dominant political force to exercise control over the Mediterranean and North Atlantic coastal seas. As various governmental entities arose and developed into modern nation-states, they individually appropriated adjacent areas of the sea for their exclusive use.[4] This was done for a number of reasons, principally to ensure the safety of coastal commerce, which was then being plagued by pirates just as overland commerce was being harrassed by highwaymen and marauding bands. Many states found other objectives to be secured in declaring significantly large ocean areas as being subject to the sole control of the coastal state. Some of the Scandinavian states, for example, levied tributes for the right of passage in order to add to their national treasuries, and England sought to protect her coastal fisheries by excluding foreigners from fishing activities in her coastal waters.

13

14

Most important for future legal developments, however, Portugal and Spain sought to impose control over the newly traversed expanses of the Atlantic and Indian Oceans for purposes of establishing a trade monopoly. These two nations had been the first to discover the "New World" and to initiate exploitation of its natural resources for their economic benefit. They were not disposed to share this new bounty with their neighboring European nations and thus sought, through a variety of mechanisms, to exclude all other nations from engaging in trade with the New World. Among other measures, Spain and Portugal enlisted the support of the Pope, who issued a series of papal bulls confirming the monopoly sought by Spain and Portugal. For example, the bull of May 4, 1493, confirmed to Spain all the newly discovered islands and lands west of a line of longitude 100 leagues west and south from the Azores and Cape Verde Islands. This document explicity forbade persons not authorized by Spain to go for the purpose of trade or any other reason to the islands or mainlands west of the described line, under penalty of excommunication.[5]

Temporally, Spain and Portugal concluded an agreement on June 7, 1494 (the Treaty of Tordesillas) that divided the New World between the two nations by a line of longitude lying 370 leagues west of the Cape Verde Islands (Figure 3-1). Spain was given the right to navigate in Portugal's portion provided Spanish

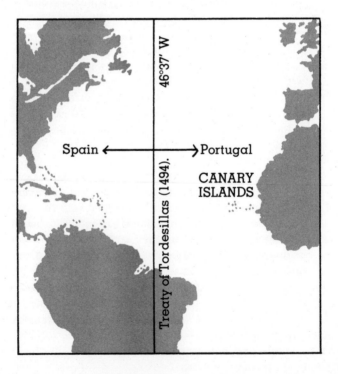

Figure 3-1. Allocation of New World Lands and Ocean Access thereto Made by Treaty of Tordesillas (1494).

ships followed the most direct route to their destination. A subsequent papal bull of January 24, 1506 approved and confirmed the Treaty of Tordesillas and instructed its inviolable observation.

By thus using their military power at sea, and by securing the support of the Pope in Rome, Spain and Portugal sought to reduce the Atlantic and Indian Oceans to the status of private lakes. Had they succeeded, the world would not only be a much different place politically than that which we know today, but the groundwork would have been laid for avoiding the tragedy of the commons for high seas fisheries through validation of the concept of national jurisdiction (limited or comprehensive) over broad reaches of ocean space. This did not occur, however, and over 400 years were to intervene before the next major attempt to reduce large ocean areas and the resources thereof to national dominion.

Emergence of the Concept of Freedom of the High Seas

Other European maritime powers—principally England and the Netherlands— were not favorably disposed to accept the bilaterally imposed division of access to the seas for trade with the New World sought by Spain and Portugal. In a noteworthy declaration, Queen Elizabeth of England stated that:

[T]his [Papal] donation of that which is another man's, which is of no validity in law, and this imaginary propriety, cannot hinder other Princes from trading into those countries and, without breach of the law of nations, from transporting colonies into those parts thereof where the Spaniards inhabit not; . . . neither from freely navigating that vast ocean, seeing the use of the sea and the air is common to all. Neither can a title of the ocean belong to any people or private persons; for as much as neither nature nor public use and custom permitith any possession thereof.[6]

Queen Elizabeth spoke with forked tongue, however, for at the same time she pronounced the doctrine of free navigation on the world ocean she was countenancing a closed sea policy with respect to fisheries in British coastal waters. It therefore becomes necessary to divorce the issues of navigation and fisheries, and to follow for the time being the evolution of the law of the sea with respect to navigation, for with limited modifications this ultimately also became the law governing high seas fisheries.

The seed of the concept of freedom of the high seas lay in the challenge of Spain and Portugal to the other nations of Europe for the right to trade with the New World. The seed came to fruition in an incident in which a Spanish vessel, the *Catharine,* was captured on the high seas by a Dutch ship captain operating on behalf of an Amsterdam firm. A judicial prize hearing resulted in a declaration that the seizure was valid. In seeking a defense or justification for the action, a young Dutch jurist, Hugo Grotius, was called on to prepare a legal brief on the subject, which he entitled *Commentary on the Law of Prize and Booty.*[7]

Although Grotius' work did not have an impact on the immediate crisis, a portion of it was separately published in 1609 under the title *Mare Liberum*.[8] In this treatise, Grotius argued that every nation was free to travel to every other nation and to trade with it utilizing the high seas for that purpose. In a sophisticated argument Grotius pointed out that some things—food, for example—must be exhausted to be utilized and for those things ownership was necessary to use them. Other things, he noted, were not exhausted by use—the air and running water, for example—and for these ownership was unnecessary and, in Grotius' view, such resources should remain free to the use of all. He then posited that the sea fell into the second classification for two reasons: (1) it could not be reduced to possession, so that even if ownership were necessary it could not be obtained; and (2) the ocean was not exhausted by use, the wake of one vessel not constituting an impediment to the navigation of those same waters by another.

Insofar as Grotius' argument related solely to the use of the bouyant capacity of the ocean to support ships engaged in trade and transportation, and considering the status of naval forces at that time, it is difficult to dispute the premises on which Grotius based his argument in support of freedom of the high seas. The latter concept, as it was then formulated (and remains essentially formulated today) is simply that no person or nation may appropriate any part of the area of the high seas for exclusive use.

The English took exception to Grotius' argument, fearing it to be an indirect attact on their imposition of a closed sea regime with respect to nearshore fisheries. Grotius, in fact, probably had in mind only the defense of Dutch interests in navigation and trade to the New World, but if his proposition were applied on a universal basis, it could also be used to support the argument that the high seas were free for fishing and that no nation could establish closed seas beyond its shores for the purpose of effecting a national monopoly on fishery resources. Indeed, one British advocate went so far as to assert that the sea could indeed be appropriated and that the practice of nations evidenced such appropriation, citing such examples in the Middle Ages as were described above.[9]

In the so-called battle of the books that followed Grotius' publication of *Mare Liberum,* it became apparent that all parties were willing to concede coastal state control over some adjacent sea areas, principally for purposes of national defense but also for purposes of protection of fisheries. This concept ultimately ripened into the doctrine of the territorial sea, which posits that within some relatively limited distance from the coast the coastal state exercises all the attributes of sovereignty that it exercises over land, with some exceptions concerning navigation such as the right of innocent passage. Territorial sea jurisdiction, being an exercise of sovereignty, includes exclusive control over access to fishery resources located there. Although the juridical content of this zone of ocean space was not in doubt, its seaward extent was. Even today there is no international agreement specifying the maximum extent of the territorial sea, though state practice appears to be leading toward emergence of a customary international law rule of a 12-mile maximum. For now, however, we shall leave coastal states with a relatively narrow band of sovereign waters of unspecified breadth and turn attention to the development of the concept of freedom of the high seas for ocean areas beyond territorial waters.

Freedom of the High Seas as a Rule of International Law

International law has two primary sources—treaties and custom. Obviously, if two or more nations bind themselves to a particular course of action by adopting a written international agreement on a particular subject, that agreement constitutes a binding obligation for the states that are party to the treaty. The treaty itself is not "international law," of course, but simply reflects the agreed rights and duties voluntarily assumed by the parties to the treaty; the underlying "law" is the rule *pacta sunt servanda,* viz., that treaties are to be performed in good faith according to their terms. Other nations, not party to the treaty, are not bound by its terms unless those terms also constitute customary rules of international law binding on all nations.

The second primary source of international law—custom—played the dominant role in the emergence of the law of the sea and its development up to the middle of the twentieth century. For a rule of customary international law to arise, a significant number of states must engage in a practice that has the acquiescense of virtually all the nations of the world and that is carried out over a sufficient period of time for the custom to ripen into a rule of law. Further, nations so acting must do so out of a feeling of legal obligation and not mere expediency. It is difficult to determine in many cases just what a rule of customary law is or whether it exists at all, and if so, from what point in time it exists. Obviously recourse to third-party decision makers must be had, and given the absence of an international judicial system of any significance, the holdings of national courts of high repute, such as the Supreme Court of the United States, have had a significant influence in determining whether and to what extent rules of customary international law exist.

Beginning in the 18th Century there is an unbroken line of judicial authority—from both domestic and international courts—affirming the proposition that the high seas are free and open for the use of all and may not be subjected to appropriation by any individual or nation. For example, an 1817 English court decision states that "all nations being equal, all have an equal right to the uninterupted use of the unappropriated parts of the ocean for their navigation.[10] In an 1826 decision, the United States Supreme Court noted that:

Upon the ocean, then, in time of peace, all possess an entire equality. It is the common highway of all, appropriated to the use of all; and no one can vindicate to himself a superior or exclusive prerogative there.[11]

In 1927 the Permanent Court of International Justice observed that:

[V]essels on the high seas are subject to no authority except that of the state whose flag they fly. In virtue of the principle of the freedom of the seas, that is to say, the absence of any territorial sovereignty upon the high seas, no State may exercise any kind of jurisdiction over foreign vessels upon them.[12]

Finally, at the First United Nations Conference on the Law of the Sea held in Geneva in 1958, the Convention on the High Seas was adopted, Article 2 of which provides that:

The high seas being open to all nations, no State may validly purport to subject any part of them to its sovereignty. Freedom of the high seas is exercised under the conditions laid down by these articles and by the other rules of international law. It comprises, *inter alia,* both for coastal and non-coastal States:
    (1) freedom of navigation;
    (2) freedom of fishing;
    (3) freedom to lay submarine cables and pipelines;
    (4) freedom to fly over the high seas.
    These freedoms, and others which are recognized by the general principles of international law, shall be exercised by all States with reasonable regard to the interests of other States in their exercise of the freedom of the high seas.[13]

The first sentence of Article 2 reflects the Grotian concept of freedom of the high seas. It is to be noted, however, that the last sentence evidences an awareness that the intensity and diversity of the use of the ocean had increased to the point where some degree of reasonableness must be exercised in utilizing one's high seas freedoms. The seed of this modification of the Grotian doctrine had been sown by the United States Supreme Court in 1826 in a decision concerning the seizure of a Portugese vessel by an American vessel off the United States coast beyond the latter's 3-mile limit of territorial waters. In commenting on the action the Court noted that:

Every ship sails [on the high seas] with the unquestionable right of pursuing their own lawful business, without interruption; but whatever may be that business, she is bound to pursue it in such a manner as not to violate the rights of others. The general maximum in such cases is, *sic utere tuo, ut non alienum laedas.*[14]

In short, the Court said, one must exercise ocean rights so as not to impinge on the rights of others or cause damage to the property of others. This notion of something other than an absolute right of freedom on the high seas was the beginning of a new stage in law of the sea development that would have important ramifications for the emergence of international rules concerning high seas fisheries management in the latter half of the twentieth century.

Developments of Nonfishery Law

As the law of the sea continued to evolve during the eighteenth through the twentieth century, a number of jurisdictional concepts were developed that gave rise to a sometimes confusing and often overlapping series of competences with respect to the ocean and its resources. In order to fully understand the position of high seas fisheries in the whole scheme of law of the sea, it is necessary to have a brief exposure to these other concepts. In Figure 3–2, the five horizontal strata of ocean space are depicted, together with the principal uses of each area. Cutting across these strata are the various boundary lines representing the jurisdictional regimes established for particular uses of the ocean (see Figure 3–3).

The *baseline* is a line along the coast, usually the low-water mark, but also consisting of straight line segments across the mouths of bays, rivers, and other irregular coastal features.[15] There is a complex body of law concerning the location of baselines and it constitutes an important element of the law of the

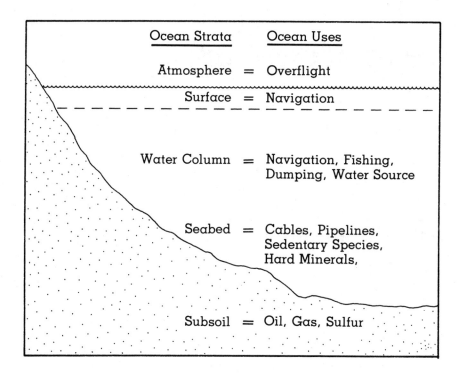

Figure 3–2. Horizontal Strata of Ocean Space and Typical Uses of Each Stratum.

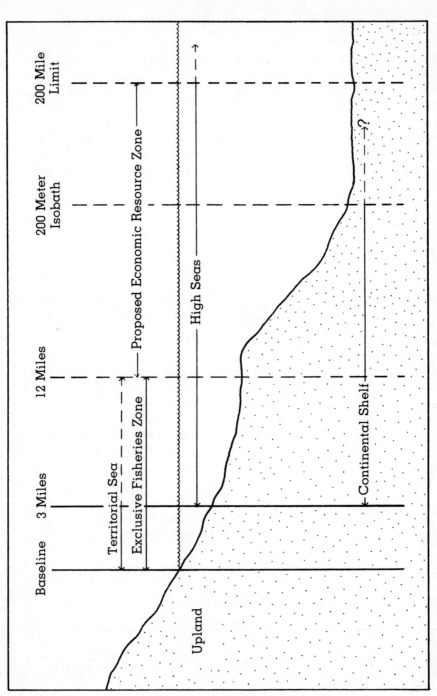

Figure 3–3. Zones of Ocean Space Jurisdiction.

Note that continental shelf jurisdiction extends only to the resources of the seabed and subsoil, while high seas jurisdiction is limited to the water column, surface, and atmosphere. The seaward extent and strata covered by a special contiguous zone are dependent on the particular claim or state practice.

sea, because it is from such baselines that all zones of ocean space based on a fixed distance from the shore are measured. For example, the territorial sea, the zone in which coastal states have virtually absolute sovereignty save for the right of navigation in innocent passage, is measured from 3 to 12 or more miles from the coast, depending on the particular national claim.

The concept of the *territorial sea,* which was discussed earlier but left in a preliminary stage of development, ripened into a rule of customary international law together with the concept of freedom of the high seas. The principle was ultimately codified in the Convention on the Territorial Sea and the Contiguous Zone, which provides that:

The sovereignty of a State extends, beyond its land territory and its internal waters, to a belt of sea adjacent to its coast, described as the territorial sea. . . .
    The sovereignty of a coastal State extends to the air space over the territorial sea as well as to its bed and subsoil.[16]

Exceptions to this exercise of sovereignty were provided in the Convention for entry in distress and for innocent passage. [17] This sovereignty includes, of course, the exclusive authority to regulate access to fishery resources and the conduct of fishery activities.

The breadth of the territorial sea has never been subject to international agreement, and it is doubtful whether state practice in modern times has ever been sufficiently consistent to provide the basis for emergence of a rule of customary international law on the subject. Both the 1958 and the 1960 United Nations meetings on law of the sea failed to produce agreement on territorial sea breadth.[18] It is important to note in this regard that the International Court of Justice held in 1951 that "[t]he delimitation of sea areas has always an international aspect; it cannot be dependent merely upon the will of the coastal state as expressed in its municipal law."[19] The statement notwithstanding, it is in fact the practice of states, each acting unilaterally, that can provide the basis from which customary rules emerge. However, even by 1956, the International Law Commission (the preparatory body for the First U.N. Conference on the Law of the Sea) could only state in its draft law of the sea articles that it "recognizes that international practice is not uniform as regards the delimitation of the territorial sea."[20] However, the Commission did note that in its opinion "international law does not permit an extension of the territorial sea beyond twelve miles."[21] According to data published by the Department of State in December 1976 (see Annex A), thirty states claim a 3-mile limit, eighteen claim between 3 and 12 miles, fifty-six claim 12 miles, and twenty-one claim over 12 miles (nine claiming 200 miles).

Beyond the territorial sea there have been established from time to time what are known as *special contiguous zones.* These zones are established for limited purposes for limited periods of time in response to some functional need (see Figure 3–3). In their seminal work on law of the sea, Professors McDougal and Burke note that:

The real function of the contiguous zone concept has been to serve as a safety valve from the rigidities of the territorial sea, permitting the satisfaction of particular reasonable demands through exercise of limited authority which does not endanger the whole gamut of community interest.[22]

Among the types of such zones that have been established in the past are those relating to customs, neutrality, national security, health, fiscal, immigration, and environmental protection.[23] Usually such zones are imposed only until the particular problem is rectified in some other manner (termination of neutrality zones as a result of conclusion of hostilities, for example) while others are widely accepted in state practice and ultimately ripen into rules of international law (a 12-mile zone for purposes of fiscal, health, sanitary, and immigration control, for example).

Most important of the contiguous zones from an economic standpoint is the *continental shelf.* This internationally accepted rule—both in its customary and its conventional form—accords to the coastal state exclusive rights to exploit the mineral resources of the seabed and subsoil in the continental shelf adjacent to its coast. These rights appertain to coastal states regardless of any claim or actual operations, and thus no nation may exploit the mineral resources of another's continental shelf. One contentious issue with regard to the doctrine of the continental shelf has been the seaward extent of such rights. In the 1958 Convention on the Continental Shelf the seaward extent was specified at the 200-meter isobath or "beyond that limit, to where the depth of the superjacent waters admits of the exploitation of the natural resources."[24] This open-ended definition gave rise to a great deal of speculation as to its precise meaning when it became clear that the technology of the oil and gas industry would soon make the 200-meter isobath depth irrelevant as a seaward boundary (see Figure 3-4).[25] It appears to be the consensus of those nations presently negotiating a new law of the sea treaty in the United Nations that the seaward extent of the continental shelf will henceforth be considered as coterminous with the edge of the physical continental margin. This means that the legal continental shelf will include physical continental shelf, slope, and rise, the latter three divisions making up what is generally referred to as the continental margin.

Even with a fixed limit to national jurisdiction over submerged mineral resources under the continental shelf doctrine, there remains the question of the legal regime to govern the exploitation of seabed minerals beyond the limit of national jurisdiction. This question is also high on the agenda in the current law of the sea negotiations. At present, those resources are considered *res nullius,* the property of no one, subject to appropriation by those who reduce them to their possession. Most of the world's underdeveloped nations are supporting development of an international seabed mining authority to govern the extraction of these resources. Developed nations seek nondiscriminatory access to seabed minerals in much the same manner as coastal states govern the extraction of oil and gas from their adjacent continental shelves. How this dispute will be resolved is at the present time uncertain.

23

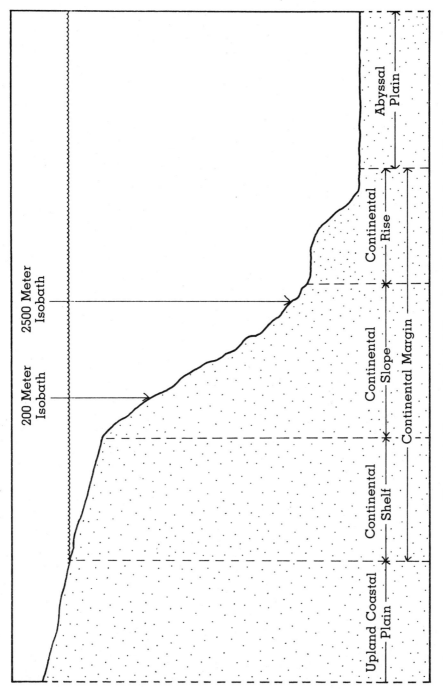

Figure 3-4. Geomorphological Characteristics of the Continental Margin.

The Impact of Freedom of the High Seas on Fisheries

Freedom of the high seas meant, insofar as fisheries were concerned, that no nation or individual could validly assert exclusive competence over fishing activities beyond the relatively narrow limits of territorial waters. The fish were considered *res nullius*—the property of no one—and were therefore subject to the law of capture. Title vested in the individual who first reduced the fish to possession. No system of property rights appertained on the high seas. Thus, one individual could expend considerable time and resources in locating a fish stock, only to have a competitor take advantage of this skill and investment by pulling alongside and joining in the good catch. It also meant that there could be no limitation on the number of fishing vessels, the number of people, or the amount of effort that they put into a given fishery. What was once an economical fishery could swiftly become uneconomical when effort reached the point that the stock was depleted below a level that could permit a harvest value in excess of the costs of fishing.

The Impact of the First United Nations Conference on the High Seas Fisheries

Held in 1958 in Geneva, the First United Nations Law of the Sea Conference produced four international agreements, each of which had some influence on the problem of high seas fisheries management. Most significantly, however, the Conference failed to agree on the precise nature of coastal states' rights in fishery resources adjacent to their coasts but beyond the territorial sea. Both of these subjects were dealt with two years later at the Second United Nations Law of the Sea Conference held in 1960 in Geneva but that Conference too was inconclusive.[26]

Convention on the High Seas

As previously noted, the Convention on the High Seas codifies the principle of freedom of fishing on the high seas while qualifying it by the rule of reasonableness in the exercise of that freedom. The Convention also specifies that land-locked states should have free access to the sea in order to exercise their right of high seas freedom of fishing but goes no further than to assert that states situated between the sea and the landlocked state should by common agreement with the latter accord the landlocked state certain rights of transit.[27]

The Convention also provides that hot pursuit of foreign ships may be undertaken for offenses committed in internal waters, the territorial sea, or the contiguous zone of the coastal state.[28] The doctrine of hot pursuit simply provides that if the pursuit is begun when the offending ship is within one of those zones, it may be continued on the high seas where a seizure may be lawfully effected. It was unclear from the language of the Convention itself whether the right of hot pursuit would apply to exclusive fishing zones beyond territorial waters. In a recent United States Federal Court case, however, the right to exercise hot pursuit from the United States 12-mile exclusive fishing zone was upheld.[29] Presumably such a right would also appertain in the new 200-mile fishing zone of the United States, to be discussed in detail in Chapter 6.

The Convention on the Continental Shelf

The Convention on the Continental Shelf provides that the coastal state exercises exclusive sovereign rights for the purpose of exploring for and exploiting natural resources in the seabed and subsoil together with sedentary species, the latter being defined as organisms that, at the harvestable stage, either are immobile on or under the seabed or are unable to move except in constant physical contact with the seabed or the subsoil.[30] The Convention thus grants to each coastal state exclusive access to and regulatory authority over the sedentary species of living resources situated on its continental shelf. The shelf extends to substantial distances from the coastline in many parts of the world, and thus limited coastal state competence to extended distances over one classification of living marine resources was recognized in 1958.

The Continental Shelf Convention also contains, in Article 6, provisions for apportioning continental shelf areas between opposite and adjacent states. The principle utilized is the equidistance formula, i.e., a line every point of which is equidistant from nearest points of the baseline. This provides a unique boundary, although it is one subject to anomalies as a result of unusual coastal configurations, the presence of islands, and so forth. Although equidistance is not considered a rule of customary international law,[31] the principle nonetheless provides the starting point for most offshore boundary negotiations and is likely to be used with increasing frequency in the case of overlapping 200-mile exclusive fishing zones.

Convention on the Territorial Sea and the Contiguous Zone

The Convention on the Territorial Sea and the Contiguous Zone contains detailed provisions with respect to the location of the baseline from which other zones of ocean space are measured. These provisions are important for fisheries since the extent of exclusive fishery zones may be significantly dependent on the location of the baseline.

More importantly, the Convention provides for a right of innocent passage for foreign vessels through the territorial waters of other states, and specifically provides that:

Passage of foreign fishing vessels shall not be considered innocent if they do not observe such laws and regulations as the coastal state may make and publish in order to prevent these vessels from fishing in the territorial sea. [32]

As previously mentioned, the Convention does not specify a breadth for the territorial sea. It does, however, provide for a 12-mile contiguous zone in which coastal states are authorized to prevent infringement of their customs, fiscal, immigration, or sanitary regulations within their territory or territorial seas, and to punish infringement of such regulations committed within their territory or territorial sea.[33]

Convention on Fishing and Conservation of the Living Resources of the High Seas

The Convention on Fishing and Conservation of the Living Resources of the High Seas[34] placed a duty on states party thereto to adopt conservation systems governing the fishing activities of their nationals engaged in high seas fisheries. Such regulations are to be adopted by negotiation if two or more states are engaged in the same fishery and, failing agreement, arbitration is to be utilized to resolve differences. New entrants to a fishery are subject to regulations in force unless they object thereto in which case arbitration is again available as a dispute settlement device. The special interest of the coastal state in fishery resources off its coast is recognized in the provision permitting coastal state involvement in regulations affecting such fisheries even though the coastal state is not engaged in the exploitation effort. The conservation objectives of the Convention are defined to be "the measures rendering possible the optimum sustainable yield from those resources so as to secure a maximum supply of food and other marine products."

The Convention has not been ratified by most nations actively involved in the high seas fishery or most nations directly concerned with fisheries conflicts, and as of this writing the dispute settlement provisions of the Convention have never been invoked.

Evolutionary Stages in the Law of the Sea[35]

Given this overview of the process by which rules relating to high seas fisheries came into existence over the past 400 years, it is appropriate at this point to put the rules into an evolutionary perspective.

All law of the sea, that relating to high seas fisheries management included, can be fitted into an evolutionary process having four stages. I suggest that the stages in this evolution are as follows: (1) unrestricted and unregulated freedom of the high seas; (2) reasonable use of the high seas; (3) regulated use of the high seas; and (4) establishment of property rights in the high seas.

Unrestricted and Unregulated Freedom

The concept of absolute freedom of the high seas, already discussed in some detail, remained the fundamental basis governing use of the sea well into the twentieth century. As long as Grotius' two premises—inexhaustibility of resources, and insusceptibility to appropriation—held true, the doctrine was a valid one in principle and a sound one in practice. However, as the assumptions of inexhaustibility and nonappropriation became invalid with respect to some uses of the sea, it became clear that some new basis of law must be adopted. In fisheries, for example, the open access character dictated by the principle led to overcapitalization, congestion of gear, and biologic depletion of fishery stocks. Likewise, the availability of venture of capital to develop offshore petroleum and natural gas depended on the establishment of some system of exclusive tenure to the ocean resources in question.

Reasonable Use

The next development was the concept of slightly limiting total freedom of the seas on the basis of a "reasonable use" theory. That is, users of the high seas were free to navigate, fish, and so forth, but were now required to exercise these rights with due regard to the interests of other nations. Although one of the first expressions of this concept came in the 1826 United States Supreme Court decision quoted above, it remained for the 1958 UN Conference on the Law of the Sea to ensconce the principle in treaty language. Pursuant to a reasonable use theory, nations could promulgate rules and regulations governing their citizens with respect to their use of the high seas but could not unilaterally affect the general rules of international law under which citizens of other nations acted. The weakness of the reasonable use approach was in determining what was, in fact, reasonable. There was no compulsory dispute settlement mechanism available, and so traditional diplomatic processes were reverted to, sometimes with quiet success, other times with violent failure. A classic example was the United States assertion of the right to conduct hydrogen bomb tests on the high seas, phrasing its legal argument in terms of the reasonableness of the action in conjunction with protection of national security.[36]

Regulated Use

The third phase—which we are just now entering—is that of "regulated use" of the high seas. This differs from reasonable use in that nations are now attempting to cope together rather than unilaterally with the problems of multiple and conflicting uses of the sea. Regulations (such as the four 1958 law of the sea treaties) are drawn up by the affected nations and become binding on parties thereto. The treaties concerning pollution promulgated by the Intergovernmental Maritime Consultative Organization (IMCO) are examples of this type of regulated use. This phase attempts to take the reasonable use theory, which is quite general in import, and apply it with specificity to a particular problem in the use of ocean space. This approach does not require general global agreement on all law of the sea issues, but simply requires that the affected states come to some specific mutual agreement that will be binding on them for the regulation of the activity in question.

There have been successes and failures in the regulatory approach. On the one hand, international fishery commissions and conventions are, by and large, now inadequate to the task of managing living resources of the sea; and the provisions in the Territorial Sea Convention concerning innocent passage through the territorial sea and straits used for international navigation are too subjective to be generative of a stable regime of navigation. On the other hand, the basic concept of the Convention on the Continental Shelf has provided the needed exclusivity of tenure to permit development of much needed fossil fuels from submerged lands (yet the boundary delimitation provisions of the same agreement are inadequate to the point that boundary disputes, in the East China Sea, for example, have halted development of some new offshore petroleum and natural gas fields).

Property Rights

The final phase in this evolutionary process will be the establishment of property rights throughout the world ocean. This may or may not become necessary with respect to all uses of the sea, but for those demanding an exclusive access and fixed tenure—such as deep seabed nodule mining, or some types of high seas fisheries—it is the inevitable result of the pressure being brought on ocean resources by the development of technology and increasing population with its attendant demand for new food and energy resources. Property rights can already be said to exist in the case of offshore hydrocarbon resources. The Convention on the Continental Shelf, as well as customary international law, accords exclusive access to coastal states to the nonliving resources off their coasts (the distance seaward, as noted above, being in contention). Coastal states then allocate exclusive tenure to public and private companies through a variety of systems. The need for such a system of property rights in international fisheries has been amply demonstrated by economists in the past twenty years. So, with any use of ocean space, when (1) overcrowding begins to result in conflict or economic waste, and (2) regulation is insufficient or unattainable, property rights will be required for rational and efficient management. The 200-mile economic resource zones are a major step in this direction, but vast areas and many uses of the ocean will remain untouched by that approach. Also at issue is whether isolated property systems are sufficient without some inter-linking set of international standards to govern the national regulation of ac-tivities within each such zone.

With this background of the development and substance of law of the sea before us, it is now time to concentrate exclusively on problems of high seas fisheries management. The concept of freedom of the high seas meant, for fisheries, that no nation could deny access to the citizens of any other nation to engage in fishing operations on the high seas, that is beyond the limit of the territorial sea, which until very recently was generally regarded as 3 miles in breadth. Freedom of the high seas thus meant "open access" to high seas fish-eries. If a particular high seas fishing ground was particularly well stocked, one might expect fishing boats from a dozen different nations, in unlimited num-bers, to converge on the fishing grounds and to engage in fishing activities vir-tually without restraint. Of course, from at least the beginning of the nineteenth century, such fishing crews were under the obligation to exercise their freedom of fishing with reasonable regard to the rights of so engaged, but this was never interpreted to go beyond a duty to avoid damaging or entangling another's gear or interfering with safe navigation. Apparently the fact that intensive fishing and overfishing would work a depletion of stock and an economic hardship on other participants was not considered unreasonable.

Notes

1. Coleman Phillipson, *The International Law and Custom of Ancient Greece and Rome* (London: Macmillan and Co., Ltd., 1911), pp. 376-378.

2. See Percy Thomas Fenn, "Justinian and the Freedom of the Sea," *American Journal of International Law* 19 (1925): 716-727, 717, 725-726.

3. Pitman Potter, *The Freedom of the Sea in History, Law and Politics* (New York: Longmans, Green and Co., 1924) pp. 27, 30-35.

4. Thomas Wemyss Fulton, *The Sovereignty of the Sea* (Edinburgh: Wm. Blackwood and Sons, 1911), pp. 3-6.

5. H. Vander Linden, "Alexander VI and the Demarcation of the Mari-time and Colonial Domains of Spain and Portugal, 1493-1494," *American Historical Review* 22 (1916): 1-20.

6. William Camden, *The History of the Most Renowned and Victorious Princess Elizabeth, Late Queen of England* (1688), p. 255.

7. George A. Finch, *Preface to DeJure Praedae Commentarius* (Oxford, England: Clarendon Press, 1950), pp. xiii–xv.

8. Hugo Grotius, *Mare Liberum* (Oxford, England: Clarendon Press, Magoffin translation, 1916), chap. 5.

9. John Selden, *Mare Clausum* (1635) summarized in Fulton, op. cit., pp. 370–374.

10. *Le Louis,* 2 Dodson 210, 165 Eng. Rpts. 1464 (1817).

11. *The Marianna Flora,* 11 Wheat. (24 U.S.) 1 (1826).

12. *The S. S. Lotus* (France v. Turkey), P.C.I.J. Series A, No. 10 (1927).

13. Convention on the High Seas, Apr. 29, 1958, 13 U.S.T. 2312 (1962), T.I.A.S. No. 5200, 450 U.N.T.S. 82 (in force 30 Sept. 1962), art. 2.

14. The Marianna Flora, op. cit.

15. Generally agreed principles of baseline delimitation are contained in articles 3–13 of the Convention on the Territorial Sea and the Contiguous Zone, Apr. 29, 1958, 15 U.S.T. 1606 (1964), T.I.A.S. No. 5639, 516 U.N.T.S. 205 (in force 10 Sept. 1964).

16. Convention on the Territorial Sea and the Contiguous Zone, op. cit., arts. 1(1) and 2.

17. See Convention on the Territorial Sea and the Contiguous Zone, op. cit., arts. 14–23.

18. See Bernard Heinzen, "The Three-Mile Limit: Preserving the Freedom of the Sea," *Stanford Law Review* 11 (1959): 597–664; Arthur Dean, "The Second Geneva Conference on the Law of the Sea: The Fight for Freedom of the Sea," *American Journal of International Law* 54 (1960): 751–789.

19. Anglo-Norwegian Fisheries Case (1951) I.C.J. 3, 132.

20. Report of the International Law Commission to the General Assembly, [1956] 2 Y.B. Int'l L. Comm'n 253, 256, UN Doc. A/3159 (1956), "Articles Concerning the Law of the Sea," art. 3(1).

21. Ibid., art. 3(2).

22. Myres S. McDougal and William T. Burke, *The Public Order of the Ocean* (New Haven, Conn.: Yale University Press, 1962), p. 76.

23. For examples, see H. Gary Knight (ed.), *The Law of the Sea: Cases, Documents, and Readings* (Washington, D.C.: Nautilus Press, 1976–1977 edition), pp. 79–132.

24. Convention on the Continental Shelf, Apr. 29, 1958, 15 U.S.T. 471 (1964), T.I.A.S. No. 5578, 499 U.N.T.S. 311 (in force 10 June 1964), art. 1.

25. See, e.g., E. D. Brown, "The Outer Limit of the Continental Shelf," *Juridical Review (N.S.)* 13 (1968): 111–146.

26. See, Dean, op. cit., arts. 2 and 3.

27. Convention on the High Seas, op. cit., arts. 2 and 3.

28. Ibid., art. 23.

29. *United States* v. *F/V Taiyo Maru,* 395 F. Supp. 413 (1975).

30. Convention on the Continental Shelf, op. cit., art 2.

31. See North Sea Continental Shelf Cases (1969), I.C.J. 3.

32. Convention on the Territorial Sea and the Contiguous Zone, op. cit., art. 14(5).

33. Ibid., art. 24.

34. Convention on Fishing and Conservation of the Living Resources of the High Seas, Apr. 29, 1958, 17 U.S.T. 138 (1966), T.I.A.S. No. 5969, 559 U.N.T.S. 285, in force, 20 March 1966.

35. The material in this section originally appeared in a paper entitled "Legal Aspects of Sea Power" prepared for a dialog at the Woodrow Wilson International Center for Scholars in February, 1975. It is reproduced here, in revised form, with permission of the Woodrow Wilson International Center for Scholars.

36. Myres S. McDougal and Norbert A. Schlei, "The Hydrogen Bomb Texts in Perspective: Lawful Measures for Security," *Yale Law Journal* 64 (1955): 648-710.

4

Problems and Potential Solutions in High Seas Fisheries Management

Major Issues in International Fisheries Management[1]

None of the management problems of international fisheries can be effectively addressed until there exists a jurisdictional base for management, but it is important to identify and discuss such problems at this stage since the management problems themselves contribute to an understanding of the alternatives for creating appropriate jurisdictional arrangements. Major problems of international fisheries management fall into three classifications (see Table 4-1). First, *objectives* of fisheries management must be established. Second, a system for *conservation* of fishery resources must be selected, this being essentially a scientific function but one having legal and political overtones. Third, a method of *allocation* of fishery resources among competing nations and fishermen must be adopted. The allocation problem is at the crux of all high seas fishery management conflicts for it is the question of "who gets what" from the fishery.

A brief look at some of the concepts involved in these three categories of interest is warranted before proceeding to a more detailed discussion of exclusive fishing zones, international fishery commissions, and, in the next chapter, current attempts to resolve the fishery management problem through international and judicial and legislative efforts as well as through national legislation.

Objectives of Fisheries Management

As noted, one must have jurisdiction, that is, the power to impose laws and regulations, before it makes sense to talk about objectives of fisheries management. The discussion in this section, then, is predicated on some form of jurisdictional authority being vested in a nation or a group of nations with power to affect the fishery in question.

The number of interests that could be served in a particular fishery management system is almost infinite. At the national level a country might simply be interested in maintaining a viable fishing industry and therefore have as its objective the subsidization of that industry without regard to the effect on the fishery stock. Again, a nation with a protein shortage might focus on the objective of intensified fishing effort in order to provide increased protein supply through either direct catch or through import of fishery products from other nations. Depending on the particular economic, social, and technological capabilities of the country involved, any one or combination of such national

33

Table 4-1
Major Issues in International Fisheries Management

Objectives of Fisheries Management
  Maximization of food production; conservation
  Maximization of net economic return
  Optimum yield
  Avoidance of international conflict
  Maximum utilization of the fishery for employment purposes
  Equitable allocation of fishery resources
  Development of knowledge and technology
  Minimization of Interference with other uses of ocean space
  Political acceptability
Conservation
  Determination of maximum or optimum sustainable yield
  Machinery for administration
  Enforcement mechanisms
  Costs of management
Allocation
  Distant-water versus coastal fishing nations
  New entrants
  Abstention
  Open access or allocation of rights
  Machinery for administration
  Anadromous species
  Wide-ranging species
  Sedentary species
  Role of landlocked nations

objectives could be sought through a fisheries management program.

At the international level, however, there are a limited number of major objectives in developing a rational fisheries management plan, and these tend to be the overriding considerations even in cases of exclusive fishing zones proclaimed by a single nation.

Maximization of Food Production; Conservation. A commonly asserted goal of international fisheries management is the maximization or optimization of food production from the sea. This objective was expressly recognized in the Convention on Fishing and Conservation of the Living Resources of the High Seas, which provides in Article 2:

As employed in this Convention, the expression "conservation of the living resources of the high seas" means the aggregate of the measures rendering possible the optimum sustainable yield from those resources *so as to secure a maximum supply of food and other marine products.* Conservation programs should be formulated with a view to securing in the first place a supply of food for human consumption.[2] (Emphasis added).

Most multilateral fisheries agreements also reflect this objective. Within the scope of this general objective, one can advocate short-term maximization of food production, in which a stock is fished to the point where the size of the catch does not warrant further expenditures of labor or capital, either with or without assurance that it will reconstitute itself over a period of years. This objective—the so-called pulse fishing approach—has never been formally asserted as the basis for management in any agreement, and although there is evidence that some states (principally those supporting sophisticated distant-water fishing fleets) engage in the practice, it has never been asserted as a matter of national policy.

The usual expression for this objective is securing maximum sustainable yield (MSY), reflecting the goal of providing a recurring, long-term source of food from the ocean, based on the renewable resources characteristics of the fishery (see Chapter 2). Implementing the goal of MSY presents some practical problems, however.

First, it is often difficult to define with accuracy the MSY of a given fish stock because of variations in environmental conditions and other factors. Second, two or more fishery stocks may be closely interrelated, and it is sometimes difficult to predict the effect of a particular practice with respect to the catch of one stock on the sustainable yield of another. Third, the objective of producing MSY does not take into consideration the net economic return from the enterprise and, according to some economic theorists, automatically diminishes economic return.

Maximization of Net Economic Return. A more recently suggested objective is securing the greatest economic value possible from the fishery, taking into consideration all costs of operations. This objective has not yet been implemented in any agreement or in practice, with the possible exception of arrangements concerning fur seals, but it is increasingly being urged as the only valid objective for fisheries management. Generally stated as "maximizing the net economic revenues of the sea," this goal would transfer to other spheres the extra, uneconomic effort expended in maximizing sustained yield (see Chapter 2, Figure 2-3, and accompanying text).

Among the costs often sought to be minimized in this approach are not only those of operations, but also those imposed by the competitive, open access characteristic of the high seas. Among costs not generally discussed in this respect are costs of management, i.e., the costs of staffing and operating the requisite national or international management organization.

One must also realize that maximization of economic return may not be the most desirable objective in particular situations. For example, it may be desired in certain countries to intensify the employment opportunities in fisheries in order to accomplish national employment objectives. In this case, the government may be willing to bear subsidy costs by allowing the industry to operate at less than maximum efficiency in order to secure the objectives of high employment.

Optimum Yield. A blending of the two previous objectives, with the addition of others, has been suggested under the rubric "optimum yield." That term has been defined as "a deliberate melding of biological, economic, social, and political values designed to produce the maximum benefit to society from a given stock of fish."[3] This concept permits decision makers to adopt different yield objectives for different fisheries. Under such a system, objectives might include anything from maximum sustainable yield, to zero harvest, to maximum net economic return, to exceeding maximum sustainable yield for limited periods of time, and so on.

The principal problem with this objective is controlling administrative discretion in selecting objectives for particular fisheries. If the enabling legislation is quite broad—"optimum yield" as defined above—then the administrator has total flexibility but perhaps too little accountability. In turn, if the statute is too restrictive—e.g., specifying only maximum sustainable yield, then the public will, expressed in the legislative act, is clear, but the administrator lacks desirable flexibility to cope with changing biological, environmental, and economic factors.

Avoidance of International Conflict. The United Nations Charter contains a prohibition against the use or the threat of the use of force in the conduct of international relations.[4] Resource management systems that are prone to produce conflict are clearly contrary to the theory (if not the practice) of the international order that has evolved since World War II. Another objective of international fisheries management, then, would be to design a regime that will minimize the possibilities for international conflicts.

Although relatively isolated, there are several examples of conflicts that have escalated to violence in fishery situations. These have occurred in the Iceland–United Kingdom dispute over fishing rights in waters adjacent to the coast of Iceland; in the South Pacific between Chile, Ecuador, and Peru, on the one hand, and the United States, on the other; between France and Brazil over the lobster fishery off the coast of Brazil; and between Japan and the Soviet Union with respect to sedentary species of living resources on the northwest Pacific Ocean seabed. Such conflicts often arise as a result of extensive claims of coastal state competence being challenged by fishing crews from distant-water fishing states. In other instances disputes have arisen over the question of whether particular species fall within the legitimate competence of the coastal state under the sedentary resources provision of the Convention on the Continental Shelf.

The primary concern in this objective should not so much be the physical danger from the isolated instances of violence arising from such conflicts, but rather the poisoning effect that such continuing conflicts have on international relations among the states involved. For example, the personal injuries and property damage resulting from the entire history of the United States dispute with Chile, Ecuador, and Peru in the South Pacific probably do not approach that from automobile accidents in a large city on a single day. Yet the conflict has affected United States-Latin American relations involving countries other than Chile, Ecuador, and Peru; it has been a thorn in the side of negotiators on issues other than fisheries; and it has created internal political difficulties far out of proportion to the economic values involved. Thus, in considering this objective, one must look beyond the immediate conflict manifestations, and determine the long-range effects of a failure to come to grips with situations generative of conflict.

This objective of fisheries management also goes beyond the mere inclusion in any international or regional agreement of dispute settlement provisions, and relates to the substance of the regime agreed upon, for unless the substance deals with the past conflicts and develops a system to avoid their repetition, conflict settlement provisions will be relatively worthless.

Equitable Allocation of Fishery Resources. Another possible goal of international fisheries management is the distribution of fishery resources based on some criteria other than the open access principle or coastal state preferences. Such criteria might include protein deficiency, general economic underdevelopment, or population.

Although this alternative seems to have little promise on an international scale because of the logistics involved, if considered in a narrow regional context or even in the context of bilateral or multilateral agreements, it might have some validity. Difficulties, of course, would include securing agreement on the criteria determining allocation and in making allocations pursuant to those criteria.

Development of Knowledge and Technology. Still another objective of international fisheries management could be the development of knowledge and technology through the management system in order to (1) increase biologic output, (2) increase economic efficiency, or (3) develop new resources. As noted in a subsequent section, one of the functions of most fisheries commissions is to perform scientific research and make determinations about the stocks of fish with which it is concerned in order to maximize biologic output. However, few if any commissions to date have been concerned with increasing economic efficiency or developing new resources from the sea.

Minimization of Interference with Other Uses of Ocean Space. This objective differs from the objective of avoidance of international conflict in that the latter has as its goal the reduction of conflict between states or individuals involved in fishing activities while the objective now under discussion has as its goal the avoidance of conflict between fishing activities and other uses of the marine environment.

Such conflicts can be classified in two categories—conflicts over space, and effects on the fishery resource itself. In the former would be such activities as the emplacement of artificial structures on the continental shelf for petroleum and natural gas exploitation, naval maneuvers and other sea-based military operations, general maritime navigation, and recreational activities. In the second category would be pollution or intentional modification of the marine environment.

In each of these cases, as well as others, it may be desirable to develop the concept of multiple or compatible use rather than limiting the use of a particular area of ocean space to a single endeavor. Thus, another objective of an international fisheries management system might be to ensure that the activities carried on by the fishing industry are not inconsistent with other traditional uses of the areas involved, and vice versa.

Political Acceptability. This objective differs from the others in that it does not go to the substance of an international fisheries management regime as such but rather to perceptions about that substance held by members of the international community. Any international fisheries regime must, in order to be effectuated, be acceptable to a substantial majority of nations (perhaps a two-thirds majority if the route of international agreement in the context of a global conference is utilized). This acceptability will itself depend on the perceptions of coastal states about their national interests in international fisheries management. It is important that in considering objectives to be optimized in a given regime, the positions and interests of these nations be taken into account, for the technically most desirable regime would be worthless in practical effect if it lacks political acceptability.

It should be noted, however, that acceptability can be as much a matter of education as of perception. In ensuring acceptability, then, an objective of fisheries management regimes might be the education of decision makers in all nations concerning the scientifically determinable facts about fishery stocks, the technology for their harvest, and the economics of their consumption. What would be politically unacceptable today because of ignorance of the facts could become feasible tomorrow through logical explanations of the workings of the international fishery.

Conservation

As noted earlier, conservation refers to the objective of ensuring a renewable yield from a resource stock.[5] No matter which objective or blend of objectives are selected for managing a particular fishery stock, conservation efforts are always required, for without maintenance of a recurring stock there will be no resource with which to deal. Although most conservation efforts have in the past been directed at the objective of MSY, this should not obscure the fact

that even if the objective is maximization of net economic return, certain conservation practices must be followed, including measures to ensure that MSY
is not exceeded. This concept, which is also at the core of the goal of maximizing food production from the sea, has several aspects.

Determination of Maximum or Optimum Sustainable Yield. Determination of
MSY involves the gathering of basic scientific data about fishery stocks—their
migratory patterns, breeding habits, natural predation, and other factors. The
object is to determine for a given time period the amount of fish that can be
harvested from a particular stock while ensuring a similar return from the stock
in future time periods. Two of the issues involved in this effort are of particular
importance.

First, there is in some situations a difficulty in determining sustainable yield
figures because of complex interrelationships among various species of fish in
a given area. These interrelationships are sometimes not well understood and
present serious obstacles to data analysis. Suppose, for instance, that the maximum sustainable yield for two interrelated stocks of fish, A and B, were set
at 2000 and 5000 units, respectively, on the basis of research on the species in
isolation. Assume further that stock A is a predator of stock B. If stock B is
fished at the maximum sustainable yield of 5000 units, this will cause a reduction in food supply for stock A, which could result in diminution of its total
mass. That being the case, the figure of 2000 units as maximum sustainable
yield for stock A, although correct on an isolated analysis, would at that point
probably be excessive. A further difficulty—related to the actual catching process rather than the theoretical determination of an acceptable figure—is that
of "incidental catch." Even if acceptable sustainable yield figures can be developed, ensuring adherence to the limit is difficult in practice because of the
incidental harvest of stocks and the unreliability of data on this practice.

Second, raw data are always subject to interpretation, and, as with the interpretation of geophysical data concerning fossil fuel deposits in submerged
lands, there can be as many interpretations of fisheries data as there are interpreters. In the fisheries situation the issue is further complicated by the fact
that national interests are at stake, and one can at least question the impartiality
of the interpreters of data when the positions of their respective nation-states
may depend on the outcome of the analysis. Naturally, one is loath to suggest
any lack of impartiality on the part of scientists, but within the confines of a
given discipline there are always doctrinal disputes and much room for variation
in interpretation, so that given the present system of fishery commissions there
may be some problems associated with the nation-state approach to fisheries
management.

Machinery for Administration. The application of conservation systems with
respect to high seas fisheries requires some national, regional, or international

machinery that can (1) conduct the research necessary for establishing standards, (2) make recommendations based on that research, and (3) exercise the requisite enforcement authority with respect to such recommendations. The principal issue is the locus in the world governmental hierarchy of this authority—national, regional, or international.

If 200-mile exclusive fishing zones are adopted, it would seem that such machinery would probably be relegated to the category of national level. However, a distinction can be made between the administration of regulations, on the one hand, and their adoption and enforcement, on the other. Regulations concerning high seas fisheries even within an exclusive fisheries zone could be made at an international or regional level and subsequently administered on a national level provided, of course, that the nation-state concerned consented to the supranational elements. However, it is more likely that the 200-mile exclusive economic zone will result in essentially national machinery or the adoption and implementation of national management systems. This, of course, ignores the biologic realities of the migratory patterns of fish, which would dictate in most cases that some form of regional or multilateral management system be effected.

There is also a good deal of support in the current international law of the sea negotiations for regional approaches to high seas fisheries management on the basis that certain stocks are more closely connected with limited regions than they are with the entire world ocean and that local problems and local expertise dictate regional solutions rather than some international organization far removed from the locale of the fishery. Of course, some overall international machinery could be desirable from the standpoint of adopting rather general, fundamental standards for the conduct of fisheries regulation concerning such areas as avoidance of international conflict and minimization of interference with other uses of ocean space. These types of objectives, if left at the regional or national level, might be unattainable due to national or regional conflicts. Finally, one must also consider that there already exist some twenty international fishery management bodies, and it may be desirable to develop a new system utilizing these existing mechanisms rather than simply scrapping them.

Enforcement Mechanisms. As will be noted with respect to existing fishery commissions and agreements, the problem of enforcement has been a serious deterrent to effective fisheries management. Thus a critical aspect of any conservation system is the development of a mechanism by which the standards adopted can be enforced in practice. This, of course, requires concessions on the part of nations concerning aspects of their sovereignty with respect to territorial water areas, economic resource zones, or their citizens. In given situations this may be more or less difficult to achieve. For instance, virtually all nations have refused to accept any enforcement mechanisms external to their own national interests.

Costs of Management. Little consideration has been given in the past in analyzing the effectiveness of fishery management systems in terms of the costs involved in the management system itself. These costs include the salaries paid to staffs of fishery commissions, funds allocated for special studies, supplies and equipment necessary to carry out scientific investigations, and the economic outlay to generally administer and enforce such agreements. If in fact such costs result in a negative economic return from a particular stock, it is questionable whether the management effort itself is an acceptable goal. On the other hand, one must compare to that situation one in which there is no regulation and concomitant overfishing and destruction of the fishery stock. The costs in the latter case may outweigh the ultimate costs even though there is a heavy burden from management.

Allocation

As previously noted, allocation concerns the issue of the distribution of the catch or revenue therefrom among participants or nonparticipants in the fishery.[6] There are a number of existing or proposed allocation mechanisms of which the most basic are *open access,* where resources are allocated to the nation or individual that first reduces them to its possession, and *coastal state preference,* where allocation is made essentially on the basis of proximity to land-based populations. The open access system places a premium on technological development, since the more sophisticated and efficient the gear, the larger the catch. Virtually all the issues concerned with allocation discussed in ths section arise from efforts to modify or restrict the effect of the open access system. Of course, the method of allocation should logically follow from the objectives of management selected, but without clearly defined objectives, all these issues are of relevance.

Distant-Water versus Costal Fishing Nations. At the core of the allocation dispute between coastal and distant-water fishing nations is the open access character of the high seas fishery. In recent years several nations have subsidized their fishing fleets and have developed sophisticated, efficient gear with which to roam the world oceans in pursuit of fish stocks. Beyond the limits of a territorial sea or recognized exclusive fisheries zone, these fleets are free to exploit fishery resources even though coastal states may also have an interest in those stocks. The issue is not clear-cut in favor of allocating the resource to either party. There are a number of factors involved.

Historic Rights. One issue concerns "historic fishing rights," which may be claimed by either coastal or distant-water fishing nations through long usage of a particular area of the high seas for the purpose of taking fishery resources. For example, when the United States adopted a 12-mile exclusive fisheries zone in 1966, traditional fishing rights of citizens of Mexico, *inter alia,* in the 3- to 12-mile belt were recognized and handled on a "phase out" basis. This in itself does not constitute any explicit recognition that Mexico had *legal* rights in the fisheries in this zone, but does reflect the fact of political and economic life that it would be generative of conflict to eliminate suddenly and unilaterally either the distant-water state or the coastal state from an area in which it had traditionally derived resources and revenues.

It must be emphasized, however, that there is no international legal doctrine of *historic fishing rights.* The concept of *historic waters* relates to the acquisition by a nation of absolute sovereignty (as opposed to mere fishing rights) over water areas adjacent to its coast where the geographical configuration (usually a bay) and past practice make it clear that the waters are not high seas. This requires not only an exercise of sovereignty by the coastal state (not merely fishing), but also a continuous display of that sovereignty and the acquiescence of other nations. Thus the operations of foreign fishing vessels off the coasts of the United States, even though continuing over a long period of time and without objection by the United States because of the high seas character of the waters beyond twelve miles from the coast, does not give rise to internationally recognizable legal rights.

Bilateral Agreements. One method of handling the conflict between distant-water and coastal fishing nations with respect to allocation of the resource has been to enter into bilateral agreements by which one party trades off certain interests or rights for another. Some of these agreements concern reciprocal access, some relate to closing of open access areas in return for opening of closed access areas, while still others contain trade-offs completely external to the fishery.

Exclusive Fishing Zones. The solution of allocation adopted (or preferred) by some nations is to establish zones of exclusive fishing rights extending to substantial distances in the sea. Such zones could be utilized to completely exclude distant-water fleet fishing activities or as a basis for regulating all fishing effort. This approach is less than satisfactory from the view of distant-water states, which tend to fear abuse of the "exclusive" privilege and prefer to base their arguments on either an erroneous case of "historic rights" or on the conclusion of special bilateral and multilateral agreements involving tradeoffs for the maintenance of their fishing rights.

New Entrants. One method of managing fishery stocks is for all the states concerned with the exploitation of that fishery to agree on maximum sustainable yield (or other objectives) and on an allocation of the resultant catch among themselves. A problem is created, however, when a new state, not previously engaged in the fishery, also wishes to exploit that stock. Because of the open access character of the high seas and the resources thereof, there is no international legal principle to prevent the new entrant from entering the fishery. However, this entry usually renders ineffective the conservation and allocation system agreed on by the parties to the agreement. There have been several proposals for handling the problem of new entrants, one of which is to allocate a certain percentage of the sustainable yield for new entrants on an annual basis. Quotas would then be adjusted to reflect the new participant. Still another proposal is that new entrants be "bought off" by those states affected through revenues generated from the fishery. With one nonrelevant exception, neither of these systems has ever been utilized in practice, and the problem of the new entrant is likely to become more severe in the next two decades as a result of developing countries' emphasis on fishery industries coupled with technical assistance from F.A.O. and other organizations.

Abstention. An issue related to that of new entrants is the "doctrine" of abstention.[7] This concept would require a state not previously engaged in a fishery to abstain from entering into that fishery if it were subject to a conservation and allocation system pursuant to international agreement. It can also refer to the concept that a state will refrain from taking anadromous species on the high seas to ensure adequate stock return to spawning grounds subject to coastal state management systems.

In fact, the doctrine of abstention is not now nor has it ever been a rule of international law. It was proposed by the United States as a method of preserving salmon and other fisheries in the Northwest Pacific Ocean. It has also been suggested as a means of handling the problem of new entrants, but, in fact, this is a nonsolution because there is no benefit to the new entrant simply from abstention. If a *quid pro quo* were found for such a situation, the result would be properly described as a bilateral (or multilateral) agreement in which one state gives up the right of access in return for another payoff, and "abstention" as such would not enter into the picture as a legal doctrine.

Open Access or Allocation of Rights. As previously noted, the open access character of the high seas and the resources thereof means that allocation is determined on a first-come-first-served basis. Opposing this system would be some mechanism for allocation of rights on the high seas much as mineral rights are allocated on an exclusive basis on the continental shelf or in upland areas.[8] This requires some governmental entity possessing the requisite jurisdiction to enforce regulations concerning limitation of entry. If 200-mile economic resource zones are adopted, each individual coastal state would then possess the requisite authority to grant rights or licenses on a stock or area basis if it so chose, although such a management system would suffer from the defects associated with species that do not remain during their entire life cycle within the jurisdiction of a single state. Beyond the limits of national jurisdiction there would have to be established an international organization that would be given powers by its constituent nations to regulate access.

In view of the traditional character of the fishery, however, there is likely to be industry resistance to such a scheme, and there will also probably be resistance from national governments (partly as a result of influence from their respective industries) to any international organization possessing the requisite jurisdiction to develop limitation of entry systems. Nonetheless, it is clear that with the continued congestion involved in productive fishing areas, some form of allocation of rights should be adopted, because completely unregulated open access results in economic and biologic waste. Whether the existing systems of bilateral or multilateral conventions will suffice is problematic.

Machinery for Administration. Many of the same issues discussed earlier with respect to conservation are involved here. The principal issue is whether the machinery for allocating the catch of a particular stock will be operative at a national, regional, or international level. Also critical is the method of allocation of rights and the decision-making process within the national, regional, or international organization. However, questions of allocation are much more politically charged than questions of conservation. Thus, it would seem likely that states would be more reluctant to give up aspects of sovereignty necessary to confer on regional or international organization the authority for allocating catch. The mechanism that has evolved in the few instances where quotas are established is simply one of international negotiation—each nation negotiates within the context of its own national priorities for the maximum allocation of the stocks in which it has the greatest interest.

It may be more desirable at some time in the future (taking into consideration the issue of political acceptability) to move this process up the ladder to regional or international organizations, which would allocate resources on the basis of specified criteria and data furnished by appropriate fishery commissions concerning conservation and catch figures.

Role of Landlocked States. The traditional interest of landlocked states in the ocean has been in securing access to the sea through neighboring coastal states for purposes of importing and exporting commodities.[9] Although arguments have been made to the effect that such a right exists as a matter of principle, no international agreement afforded to landlocked states a right to access to the sea prior to the Convention on Transit Trade of Landlocked Countries. Few coastal states have become party to this Convention, so that the plight of the landlocked state in terms of access is still essentially relegated to a question of negotiation with its coastal neighbor. Access notwithstanding, both customary and conventional international law recognize the right of all states—whether coastal or landlocked—to sail vessels on the high seas and to enjoy other freedoms of the high seas, including the freedom of fishing. Article 2 of the Convention on the High Seas makes its enumerated freedoms available "both for coastal and non-coastal states." That Convention also imposes an obligation on coastal states to negotiate in good faith with landlocked neighbors with a view toward securing access to the sea for the latter, but it does not impose any legal obligation to grant that access (Art. 3). These inhibitions notwithstanding, many landlocked nations have secured "free port" facilities in neighboring coastal states or have otherwise gained access to the sea.

With the initiation of the current law of the sea negotiations however, landlocked states have perceived new interests in the sea. First, they sought acquisition of resources and revenues from the exploitation of the nonliving resources of the deep ocean floor, beyond national limits. General Assembly Resolution 2749 recognized this interest, and it is clear that landlocked states will be provided both a political and an economic role in the development of nonliving seabed resources if a global treaty on that subject is ever adopted. Second, they have argued for a share in the resources (or revenues derived from exploitation thereof) located in the exclusive economic zone, should one be established by international agreement. To date, coastal states have shown little interest in granting landlocked states access to the oil, gas, and mineral resources of the continental shelf. Such nations have expressed sympathy, however, with the idea that landlocked states should, on a regional basis, have some rights to exploit living resources from neighboring coastal states' economic zones. Indeed, the "Revised Single Negotiating Text" produced by the Third UN Conference on the Law of the Sea at its Spring 1976 meeting in New York contains the following article dealing with landlocked nations' rights in fishery resources:

1. Land-locked States shall have the right to participate in the exploitation of the living resources of the exclusive economic zones of adjoining coastal States on an equitable basis, taking into account the relevant economic and geographical circumstances of all the States concerned. The terms and conditions of such participation shall be determined by the States concerned through bilateral, subregional or regional agreements. Developed land-locked States shall, however, be entitled to exercise their rights only within the exclusive economic zones of adjoining developed coastal states . . . .
3. Paragraph 1 is without prejudice to arrangements agreed upon in regions where the coastal States may grant to land-locked States of the same region equal or preferential rights for the exploitation of the living resources in the exclusive economic zones.

Thus, although landlocked nations are not granted a *right* to share in living resources of the economic zone, a stride will have been made in their favor should such a provision become a binding legal commitment on coastal states adjacent to landlocked nations.

Potential Solutions to the Tragedy of the Commons

As mentioned briefly in Chapter 1, there are essentially two solutions to the potential tragedy of the commons—creation of private property, or characterization of the commons as public property subject to governmental regulation as to access and use. Each of these solutions has its counterpart in international fisheries management.

As the population of the world increased and placed a concomitant demand on food resources, the intensity of fishing effort to produce consumable protein was likewise increased. Naturally, this effort was not dispersed evenly throughout the world ocean but was, as one might expect, concentrated in particular areas of high biological productivity. In fact 90 percent of the sea by area is relatively unproductive while another 9.9 percent has only moderate production (concentrated mainly above the world continental shelves). Only 0.1 percent has what could be characterized as very high productivity, these areas being where the upwelling of deep water brings life supporting nutrients to the surface. In addition to this uneven distribution of fishery resources, the tastes of human beings tend toward certain types of seafood with the result that fishing is apt to be concentrated on a few favorite species rather than simply fishing for bulk protein. Both of these factors led, even by the nineteenth century, to such an intensive fishing effort in some areas that unregulated stocks were in danger of depletion, and some were in fact depleted beyond the point of economic viability.

In the twentieth century more sophisticated fishing methods began to be developed culminating in the so-called factory ships, which could remain away from their home ports for great lengths of time, processing and freezing the catch on board. This development enabled fishing fleets to remain in a particular area for a much greater length of time, thus contributing further to the intensity with which stocks were fished.

As scientists begin to determine that the sustainable yield of many species was being exceeded and observed the actual depletion of several stocks, it became obvious that some form of regulation was necessary. However, as noted in the last chapter, the concept of freedom of the high seas was founded on the principle that no nation could appropriate—i.e., exercise jurisdiction over—any area of the high seas. Two approaches were taken to circumvent this governing principle of international law as applied to high seas fisheries.

First, some nations extended their exclusive fishing jurisdiction into the sea in contravention of the principle of freedom of the high seas. In a few cases this was achieved by simply extending the territorial sea since a coastal state's competence within that zone was nearly absolute and certainly included the right of exclusive access to fisheries located there. Others utilized the concept of a special contiguous zone for fisheries only, and left their territorial water limit at a relatively narrow distance from the coast. Most of the exclusive fishing zone claims were of limited extent, not exceeding 12 miles, but a few were cast in terms of up to 200 miles from the shore. The effect of an exclusive fishery zone is to make the adjacent coastal state the sole arbiter of who may fish for what species on what conditions within the zone. The coastal state then has the claimed power to limit access to the fishery, to establish seasons, to place conditions on the type of gear to be used, and so forth, all presumably based on sound conservation techniques that would result in a maximum or optimum sustainable yield, with the coastal state deciding what the yield should be. In this manner the concept of freedom of the high seas is eliminated in favor of exclusive management of authority in the coastal state, and the open access character of the fishery is thus done away with.

The second solution was to utilize the consensual nature of international law to regulate the activities of a few nations engaged in a particular fishery. As noted previously, states are always free to negotiate among themselves a particular course of conduct that they will follow, and they are bound vis-a-vis each other once they have become parties to such an international agreement. Of course, states that are not parties to the treaty are not bound by it. In international fisheries management this consensual approach to international law resulted in the creation of several international fishery conventions and commissions through which a group of nations interested in a specific fishery would attempt to impose some order on that fishery. For example, the United States, Japan, Canada, and the Soviet Union, might enter into an agreement with respect to the maximum sustainable yield and the allocation among the nations party to the treaty of that yield for a specific stock of North Pacific Ocean salmon. So long as the nations honored their obligations under the treaty, the concept of freedom of the high seas would have been discarded by them in this particular instance in favor of a management system that limited access for all the parties on some agreed-on and predetermined formula. Of course, if Korea decided to enter the North Pacific Ocean salmon fishery, while not becoming a party to that treaty, the treaty would probably be gutted of its significance since the Koreans, operating under the concept of the freedom of the high seas, would not be subject to any of the catch or other limitations imposed on themselves by the other four nations. Nonetheless, when new entrants are not a problem, the fishery commission/convention approach, if honored and enforced, has the same theoretical effect as assertion of exclusive jurisdiction by a single coastal state through the medium of an exclusive fishery zone.

In the remainder of this chapter we will take a closer look at the operation and effect of the two proposed solutions, i.e., exclusive fishery zones and international fishery conventions.

International Fishery Commissions[10]

International fishery agreements were utilized as early as the eighteenth century, though their use to create management mechanisms proliferated only in the 1900s, particularly after 1950. These later agreements created two basic types of institutions—research and management. The former, of which the International Council for the Exploration of the Sea (1902) and the Indo-Pacific Fisheries Council (1948) are examples, engaged only in the gathering and dissemination of scientific information that formed the data base for rational fisheries management.

Management (or regulatory) fishery organizations, of which there are now more than twenty, possess a wide range of powers and functions.[11] A few are species oriented (for example, with respect to tuna and whales) while most cover selected fishery resources within a designated area. Some species-oriented bodies are also limited in geographical area.

All fishery regulatory organizations have as their basic task the gathering and analysis of scientific data on fishery stocks in order to promote more rational management. However, the regulatory powers of such entities vary greatly. Most have only the authority to make recommendations to their member states concerning appropriate conservation action, which may include the establishment of seasons, restrictions on the use of gear, and the like. A few have power to bind their member states directly, such as the North Pacific Fur Seal Commission, which has the authority to open and close seasons. Still other commissions may issue recommendations that become binding in the absence of objections by member states within a prescribed time limit.

Enforcement of fishery commission recommendations has always presented a difficult problem, for the only jurisdiction over such activities is that of the state whose flag the fishing vessel flies. Nation-state interests have tended to dominate the multinational concern about maintenance of fishery stocks and, with lax or nonexistent enforcement, states have tended to follow their own short-term economic interests with the net result that the fishery stocks in question have often received little if any material assistance in terms of their ability to sustain an annual yield.

The conservation commission concept, although imperfect, had by and large accomplished its objectives until recent years. In the past ten years unrestrained increases in fishing effort have seriously reduced the stocks of certain important coastal stocks of fish in several parts of the world in spite of the conservation regulations. It seems abundantly clear that some new device is needed— a means of controlling fishing effort and effectively enforcing regulations on all those fishing common resources. Nonetheless, the conservation commission concept marked the turning point in the treatment of fishery resources from their consideration as prey to be hunted to a concept that considers fishery resources a renewable resource that is exhaustible and needs careful management.

Extended Exclusive Fishery Zones

A second potential solution to the tragedy of the commons for high seas fisheries is for individual nations to assert exclusive management competence over a sufficiently broad area of ocean to encompass the species of interest to that nation. Such a claim usually takes the form of an "exclusive fishing zone," but in some cases nations have asserted competence beyond that necessary to regulate fisheries in terms of an outright territorial sea. In either case, however, what the claiming nation has done is to establish a "jurisdictional base for management." In short, the nation has asserted competence to promulgate and enforce rules of law with respect to fishing activities in the geographical area claimed, a right which it would not possess under the concept of freedom of the high seas (see Annex A for a table of national claims to fishery zones).

The Legal Nature of Government Interest in Fish. Although some fishing zone claims are cast in terms of "ownership" of the fish, this is in fact a misstatement of the governmental authority with respect to free-swimming fish. Leaving aside for the moment the question of the international legal validity of the assertion of exclusive management authority or other form of jurisdiction, it is important to inquire precisely what it is that is being claimed by the government. The United States Supreme Court dealt with this issue in a number of cases involving state claims to own or manage resources within the territorial waters of the United States. The last word of the Supreme Court on the matter, which is an accurate reflection of the relationship between a claiming government and the resource in a claimed fishery zone, was:

The whole ownership [of fish] theory, in fact, is now generally regarded as but a fiction expressive in legal shorthand of the importance to its people that a State have power to preserve and regulate the exploitation of an important resource.[12]

Perhaps the most eloquent statement of the nature of a government's interest in fishery resources was made by the reknowned United States jurist Roscoe Pound:

We are also tending to limit the idea of discovery and occupation by making *res nullius* (e.g., wild game) into *res publicae* and to justify a more stringent regulation of individual use of *res communes* (e.g., of the use of running water for irrigation or for power) by declaring that they are the property of the state or are "owned by that state in trust for the people." It should be said, however, that while in form our courts and legislatures seem thus to have reduced everything but the air and the high seas to ownership, in fact the so-called state ownership of *res communes* and *res nullius* is only a sort of guardianship for social purposes. It is *imperium*, not *dominium*. The state as a corporation does not own a river as it owns the furniture in the state house. It does not own wild game as it owns the cash in the vaults of the treasury. What is meant is that conservation of important social resources requires regulation of the use of *res communes* to eliminate friction and prevent waste, and requires limitation of the times when, places where persons by whom *res nullius* may be acquired in order to prevent their extermination. Our modern way of putting it is only an incident of the nineteenth-century dogma that everything must be owned.[13]

Although the "ownership" terminology still prevails in some judicial decisions, [14] the essential point is that governmental regulatory authority with respect to free-swimming fish precludes any acquisition of an individual private property interest in those fish until they are reduced to possession in accordance with laws and regulations in force at the time.

Given, then, that the claim of an exclusive fishing zone amounts to an assertion of *regulatory authority* over the fish in place rather than a form of outright ownership, we will turn briefly to three examples of the use of exclusive zones and their impact on the nations involved.

The "Tuna War". In 1945, at the same time that the United States initiated the continental shelf doctrine through a Presidential proclamation, another Presidential initiative asserted the right of the United States to establish explicitly bounded conservation zones in high seas areas on the condition that where fishing activities involved nationals of other countries such zones were to be established only pursuant to agreement between the United States and other affected states.[15] The proclamation recognized similar rights for other nations, provided that the interests of the United States fishermen operating off their coasts were similarly recognized. Issuance of the two proclamations at the same time created some confusion, however, as to precisely what was being claimed in terms of mineral and living resources. Further, several Latin American nations with little or no physical continental shelf argued that if an industrialized nation such as the United States, heavily dependent on petroleum, were entitled to claim exclusive rights to the oil and gas and submerged lands off its coasts to substantial distances, then the underdeveloped countries with a need to feed their populations should likewise be entitled to assert jurisdiction over living resources to substantial distances from their coasts. Beginning in the late 1940s, therefore, several Latin American states extended exclusive fishing zones, or what were in some instances characterized as "territorial seas," to 200 miles from their coasts. In 1952, Chile, Ecuador, and Peru signed an international agreement in which those three countries resolved to preserve and make available to their respective peoples the natural resources of areas of sea within 200 nautical miles from their coasts and the coasts of their islands. In justifying the claim, the tripartite declaration provided that:

Owing to the geological and biological factors affecting the existence, conservation and development of the marine fauna and flora of the waters adjacent to the coasts of the declarant countries, the former extent of the territorial sea and contiguous zone is insufficient to permit the conservation, development and use of those resources, to which the coastal countries are entitled.[16]

The Peruvian government, for example, issued Presidential Decree No. 781 on August 1, 1947, claiming sovereignty over both the continental shelf and a zone of superjacent waters extending 200 miles from the coast. The United

States government protested the action of the Peruvian government. Beginning in the 1950s, Peru, Chile, and Ecuador seized a number of United States tuna vessels fishing within their 200-mile zones. Although the United States strongly protested these actions, it never resorted to arming the vessels or providing naval escorts for them. Rather the United States took a rather circuitous route in order to protect its international legal position that exclusive fishing rights should not exceed the three-mile limit. This method took the form of enactment of the Fishermen's Protective Act, adopted by Congress in 1954.[17] Basically that Act provided that if a United States vessel is seized in waters which the United States regards as high seas for a violation of a claimed exclusive fishing zone, the United States Government will reimburse *to the fishermen* any fines levied against them by the coastal state. The United States then seeks to deduct from foreign assistance granted to that coastal state the amounts of any fines so reimbursed. However, the Act contains a provision allowing the President to void any such deduction if he determines that it would not be in the national interest to do so, a practice which has been uniformly followed. Thus, the United States, by offering an economic subsidy, encourages tuna vessels to continue to fish in the claimed waters off Ecuador and Peru, thus maintaining a presence there which challenges the validity of the claimed zones. The result of this practice has been the "tuna war" that has flared from time to time, not in a few instances as a response to domestic political problems in the affected Latin American countries.[18]

The "Cod War". A second major conflict has occurred in the North Atlantic Ocean under the rubric of the "cod war."[19] In 1958, Iceland extended its exclusive fishery zone from 4 to 12 miles producing a confrontation with the United Kingdom whose citizens had traditionally fished in this area. The Icelandic proclamation followed the failure of the First UN Conference on the Law of the Sea to resolve the question of the breadth of the territorial sea or the rights of coastal states in adjacent waters. A protracted dispute followed, resulting on occasion in violence, but it was finally settled in 1961 by an exchange of notes constituting a tacit acceptance of the 12-mile zone by the British and referring any future extension of the zone to the International Court of Justice for adjudication. In 1972, Iceland extended its fishing zone from 12 to 50 miles, thus precipitating another round in the "cod war." Finally, in 1975 Iceland further extended her zone from 50 to 200 miles, precipitating the gravest crisis in the history of the cod war, threatening the NATO alliance and the presence of the U.S. airbase at Keflavik, Iceland. The attempted resolution of this dispute by the International Court of Justice and its ultimate settlement by agreement will be discussed in Chapter 5.

The U.S.-Brazil Shrimp Agreement. The third and last example of the effects of an extended fishery zone concerns the 200-mile territorial sea proclaimed by Brazil in 1970. Shrimping vessels of the United States had fished off the Brazilian coast for many years prior to the claim and rather than resort to another tuna war type situation, the two nations quickly negotiated a treaty by which United States shrimpers are allowed to fish in Brazilian waters in restricted numbers, while the United States pays an amount of money from the license fees that it collects from qualifying shrimping vessels to Brazil to enable the latter nation to engage in conservation measures with respect to those resources and to ensure enforcement of its regulations.[20] The original agreement became effective in 1973 and although designated for only a two-year term has been subsequently extended for an additional two years. Nonetheless, this obviously is a stop-gap measure pending ultimate resolution of the type of jurisdictional regime which will be adopted either through the Law of the Sea Conference or unilateral state action to manage high seas fisheries.

Notes

1. This section was originally published in H. Gary Knight (ed.), *The Future of International Fisheries Management,* © 1975 by the American Society of International Law. It is reproduced here, in revised form, with permission of the American Society of International Law.

2. Convention on Fishing and Conservation of the Living Resources of the High Seas, Apr. 29, 1958, 17 U.S.T. 138 (1966), T.I.A.S. No. 5969, 559 U.N.T.S. 285, in force, 20 March 1966, art 2.

3. Philip M. Roedel, "A Summary and Critique of the Symposium on Optimum Sustainable Yield," in Philip M. Roedel (ed.), *Optimum Sustainable Yield as a Concept in Fisheries Management* (Washington, D.C.: American Fisheries Society, 1975), p. 85.

4. UN Charter, art. 2, para. 4. ("All Members shall refrain in their international relations from the threat or use of force against the territorial integrity or political independence of any state, or in any other manner inconsistent with the Purposes of the United Nations.") State practice since 1945 has, of course, been quite to the contrary.

5. See generally D. H. Cushing, *Fisheries Resources of the Sea and Their Management* (London: Oxford University Press, 1975); and J. A. Gulland, *The Management of Marine Fisheries* (Seattle, Wash.: University of Washington Press, 1974).

6. See generally Hiroshi Kasahara, "Problems of Allocation as Applied to the Exploitation of the Living Resources of the Sea," in Lewis M. Alexander (ed.), *The Law of the Sea: Needs and Interests of Developing Countries* (Kingston, R.I.: University of Rhode Island, 1973), p. 94.

7. See, e. g., Soji Yamamoto, "The Abstention Principle and its Relation to the Evolving International Law of the Seas," *Washington Law Review* 43 (1967): 45-61.

8. See, e.g., *The Outer Continental Shelf Lands Act,* 43 U.S.C. §§1331–1343 (1964) (originally enacted as Act of August 7, 1953, ch. 345, 67 Stat. 462).

9. See Martin Ira Glassner, *Access to the Sea for Developing Land-Locked States* (The Hague: Martinus Nijhoff, 1970).

10. Portions of this section were originally published in H. Gary Knight, (ed.), *The Future of International Fisheries Management,* © 1975 by the American Society of International Law. They are reproduced here, in revised form, with permission of the American Society of International Law.

11. The best study of international fishery commissions is found in Albert W. Koers, *International Regulation of Marine Fisheries* [London: Fishing News (Books) Ltd., 1973]. See also "Report on Regulatory Fishery Bodies," F.A.O. Department of Fisheries, UN Doc. FID/C/138 (Rome, 1972).

12. *Toomer* v. *Witsell,* 334 U.S. 385, 402 (1948).

13. Roscoe Pound, *An Introduction to the Philosophy of Law* (New Haven, Conn.: Yale University Press, 1922), pp. 198–199.

14. See, e. g., *Washington Kelpers Association* v. *State of Washington,* 502 P. 2d 1170 (1972) and cases cited therein at p. 1173.

15. Pres. Proc. 2668, 3 C.F.R., 1943-1948 Comp., p. 68, 13 State Department Bulletin 486 (1945). See also, "Proclamations Concerning United States Jurisdiction over Natural Resources in Coastal Areas and the High Seas," *Department of State Bulletin* 13 (1945): 484.

16. Agreements between Chile, Ecuador, and Peru, signed at the First Conference on the Exploitation and Conservation of the Maritime Resources of the South Pacific. Santiago, Chile, August 18, 1952.

17. 22 U.S.C. §§1971-1979 (originally enacted August 27, 1954; 68 Stat. 883).

18. For a thorough examination of the political aspects of the "tuna war," see Bobbie B. Smetherman and Robert M. Smetherman, *Territorial Seas and Inter-American Relations* (New York: Praeger Publishers, 1974).

19. See Richard B. Bilder, "The Anglo-Icelandic Fisheries Dispute," *Wisconsin Law Review* 1973 (1973): 37-132.

20. Agreement between Brazil and the United States Concerning Shrimp, T.I.A.S. No. 7862, signed March 14, 1975 (superseding Agreement of February 14, 1973, T.I.A.S. No. 7063).

5

Current International Attempts to Resolve Fishery Problems

Factors Leading to a Reassessment of the Law of the Sea[1]

The law of the sea is not now nor has it ever been static. It has evolved in response to technological developments and the perceptions of nation-states about their economic and security needs in the ocean. Since technology is a dynamic process, and since perceptions about national interests change with changing domestic and international political, economic, and social developments, it is not surprising to find that the law of the sea has undergone a somewhat erratic development. The present manifestation of this dynamism can be found in the Third United Nations Conference on the Law of the Sea. The Conference is, however, simply a continuation of the process of dynamic evolution and does not represent a radical shift from one static system to another.

The significance of the dynamic status of law of the sea is its *uncertainty*. Any system that is dynamic possesses a certain degree of uncertainty. If the changes are slow and predictable, a condition of relative stability exists that permits a fairly accurate evaluation of reactions to present and contemplated activities. When the degree of change is rapid, a situation of relative instability exists that influences decision makers and planners and, in many instances, hampers their ability to deal rationally with problems occurring in the use of the ocean space and the exploitation of ocean resources.

These periods of relative stability and instability have existed from time to time throughout the history of the law of the sea. We are at present leaving an era of relative certainty and stability, which evolved from the principle of freedom of the high seas that dictated rules concerning the use of ocean space well in the twentieth century. We have obviously entered a period of relative uncertainty and instability evidenced, as noted above, by the current law of the sea negotiations. There are a number of reasons for this, most obviously (1) rapid technological developments in the use of ocean space and (2) changes in the world political scene.

The Impact of Technology

Technological developments have taken place with respect to a wide variety of ocean uses. In fishing, the development of factory ships and other technologically sophisticated distant-water gear has changed the picture of traditional coastal fisheries quite markedly. As noted, this distant-water presence has caused conflicts between coastal nations and the nations whose flag such technologically advanced ships fly. Further, technological developments have made it possible to fish more effectively, and with rising population and the concomitant demand for food, great pressure has been placed on stocks of fish, in some cases to the point of economic extinction.

The technology for extracting fossil fuels from beneath the sea has reached the point that traditional limits for the territorial sea or even the 200-meter isobath limit of continental shelf jurisdiction have become outdated. The question thus presented is the extent to which coastal states are entitled to exclusive jurisdiction over these resources.

The development of technology to mine minerals from the seabed at great depths (particularly in the form of manganese nodules, for their primary metal content of nickel, cobalt, manganese, and copper) has created the necessity for developing appropriate institutional and substantive regulatory arrangements to govern such activities. This, too, is a major issue in the current law of the sea negotiations.

A list of technological innovations could be extended almost indefinitely—e.g., into such fields as scientific research, pollution, navigation, or military use of the sea. Suffice it to say that the examples given indicate some of the technological developments that have caused nations to deem necessary the revision of law of the sea principles, thus ushering in an age of change and uncertainty pending the outcome of the negotiations.

The Impact of World Politics

Equally important in contributing to the new era of uncertainty is the revised world map. The underdeveloped nations that have emerged to independent status since the close of World War II now dominate the United Nations in terms of a voting majority. The so-called Group of 77, which numbers in excess of 100 developing countries, wields great power in a one-nation, one-vote system. The rules developed at the First Law of the Sea Conference in Geneva in 1958 are being challenged by these new nations, which, in many instances, have totally different perceptions about many of the issues involved in the use of ocean space. It is convenient in referring to these nations to use some new terminology, viz., the "North-South split." By the North, we refer to the industrially advanced nations of Eastern and Western Europe, the Soviet Union, the United States, Canada, Japan, and Australia. By the South we refer to the underdeveloped nations of Asia, Africa, and Latin America. Leaving aside the different technical approaches, the emphasis of the North in law of the sea matters is on *freedoms*—freedom of navigation (both commercial and military), freedom of scientific research, and freedom from pollution of the marine environment. The emphasis of the South is on *resources*–exclusive access to fish, oil, and to gas off the coast, and exclusive national management authority within a broad coastal area. The United States, for example, places high priority on securing a regime of unimpeded transit through international straits providing for submerged passage of submarines and overflight by military aircraft. Equally great concern is evidenced for maintenance of free navigation in any extended resource zones, as well as for a regime that will enhance scientific research and permit international standards to guide pollution control measures. The North does not oppose broad coastal state jurisdiction *per se* (save for those involved in distant-water fishing efforts) but wants to hedge that right by imposing obligations to protect freedoms that they seek.

The South does not object *per se* to the freedoms, but wants to regulate them strictly, on a *national* basis, in order to ensure achievement of national objectives, including the avoidance of economic dominance by the technologically advanced nations. Establishment of "sovereignty" over offshore natural resources is a sine qua non to a treaty acceptable to developing nations, and many feel that the control over ancillary activities such as scientific research, pollution, and even navigation is a necessary concomitant of that sovereignty. Further, while the North seeks legal regimes that ensure economic efficiency in the exploitation of ocean resources, the South is much more concerned with its own political participation in the new legal order, efficiency being a secondary consideration. In this context, then, it was inevitable that efforts would be made to rewrite the classic law of the sea.

The Third UN Law of the Sea Conference

Beginnings

The current round of law of the sea negotiations began for all practical purposes in the fall of 1967, when the Ambassador of Malta to the United Nations, Dr. Arvid Pardo, introduced an agenda item relating to peaceful use of the seabed to the United Nations General Assembly. Although the seabed question technically related only to the legal regime to govern exploitation of seabed mineral resources located beyond the continental shelf, the issue was quickly seized upon by underdeveloped nations as an opportunity to restructure the entire spectrum of the law of the sea ranging from navigation and oceanographic research to pollution and fisheries. The United States, the Soviet Union, and some other industrially advanced countries sought to limit the negotiations to what they termed "manageable packages," being in essence the issues of navigational rights that were of primary importance to them. The effort failed, however, and when the General Assembly created first an ad hoc and later a permanent seabed committee, it was charged with the review of the entire range of issues involved in the use of ocean space and the exploitation

58

of ocean resources (the agenda for the Third United Nations Conference on the Law of the Sea is appended hereto as Annex B).[2]

After six years of preparatory work, the General Assembly convened the Third United Nations Conference on the Law of the Sea with a procedural meeting in New York in December 1973. Substantive sessions were held in Caracas in 1974, Geneva in 1975, and twice in New York during 1976. As of this writing the Conference has yet to produce a treaty or treaties on any of the over 100 agenda items before it. Nonetheless, some observers feel that the Conference will ultimately succeed in producing agreement on articles covering, among other things, fisheries management. Even if this is not the case, the indications of national preferences expressed in the debates, as well as the various informal texts produced by the Conference to date, give a clear indication of the likely pattern of development of future customary international law of the sea with regard to fisheries should a treaty not be forthcoming. In looking at this quasi-legislative attempt to solve some problems of high seas fisheries management, then, it can be fairly concluded that whether the law ultimately develops through conventional or the customary law process, there is strong evidence to support the nature of the final outcome.

The Range of Proposals

A brief survey of some of the more important proposals for fisheries management advanced during the law of the sea negotiations will be outlined here. Emphasis will be placed, however, on a review of the "Revised Single Negotiating Text" provisions on fisheries, since this is the latest manifestation of consensus on the issue.

The "Species" Approach. Although the Executive Branch of the United States Government remained firmly opposed to the concept of a 200-mile exclusive fishing zone in the early stages of the negotiations, it soon became apparent that the economic zone concept was an idea whose time had come. Nonetheless, prior to the Caracas session, the United States attempted to meet the demands of coastal nations and of a significant segment of its own fishing industry for coastal state management authority over coastal species of fish, while at the same time placating the Defense Department in its effort to avoid the establishment of offshore zones that might be subject to the phenomena of "creeping jurisdiction" resulting in inhibitions on naval mobility. In attempting to satisfy both objectives, the United States delegation to the UN Seabed Committee developed what it referred to as the "species approach."[3] In essence this proposal would accord to coastal states jurisdiction over coastal species throughout their migratory range without designating any particular limit of a fisheries zone. Thus, the coastal state could maintain the requisite jurisdictional authority over coastal stocks, even beyond 200 miles, while at the same time there would be no zonal basis to serve as a base from which other aspects of jurisdiction could "creep" toward territorial sea status. Other aspects of the species approach proposed by the United States included:

1. The same regulatory authority over and preferential catch rights to coastal species would be applicable to anadromous species, with the preference being held by the state of origin;

2. Coastal states would be legally obliged to permit foreign fishing with respect to living resources not utilized by the coastal states, according priorities to states having historically fished in the region;

3. Coastal and anadromous species that migrate through waters adjacent to two or more coastal states would be subject to regulation by agreement among the affected states; the proposal did not, however, elaborate on the mechanism for management cooperation although it did contain sections on enforcement and dispute settlement to provide a framework for the cooperative process;

4. Highly migratory species such as tuna would be subject to regulation by international fishery organizations; and

5. The conservation management standard would be maximum sustainable yield, taking into account "relevant environmental and economic factors."

Little interest was expressed in the United States proposal, and by the time of the Caracas session in 1974 it was obvious that it was a nonstarter. Accordingly, the United States at that session expressed its conditional support of the 200-mile economic zone concept—provided that its other interests, particularly in freedom of navigation, could be met in any treaty establishing such a zone.

Distant-Water Fishing Nations' Proposals. Nations such as the Soviet Union and Japan, with substantial investments in distant-water fishing gear and considerable demand for protein were opposed throughout the early negotiations to the extension of exclusive fishery zones. Both of those nations submitted draft articles to the UN Seabed Committee with the Japanese articles providing for a concept of offshore preferential rights to *underdeveloped* coastal states up to their catch ability with preferential rights for *developed* states extending only to maintenance of locally conducted small scale fisheries.[4] The preferences envisioned by the Japanese did not include anadromous or highly migratory species. In the proposal Japan stated that it sought:

[T]o ensure that a gradual accommodation of interests can be brought about in the expanding exploitation and use of fishery resources of the high seas, without causing any abrupt change in the present order in fishing which might result in disturbing the economic and social structure of the states.

The stated objective of the Japanese approach was to achieve maximum sustainable yield of fishery resources and "thereby to secure and maintain a maximum supply of food and other marine products."

By the time of the Caracas session of the Third Conference in 1974, however, the U.S.S.R. had, like the United States, conditionally accepted the economic zone concept, and Japan was wavering.

The Exclusive Economic Zone Concept. Most of the coastal nations of the world supported from an early date a concept under which coastal states would have exclusive management authority over the living and nonliving resources in a zone extending substantial distances from the coast, usually specified at 200 miles. The economic zone concept can be viewed as simply a melding of existing coastal state rights under the doctrine of the continental shelf together with an exclusive fishing zone coterminous with the seaward extent of the continental shelf or to 200 miles if the shelf does not extend to such a distance. Under this interpretation the character of the superjacent waters would be retained as high seas.

Many underdeveloped nations, however, perceived the economic resource zone as essentially a zone of national jurisdiction, to be distinguished from the area beyond 200 miles, which would be an international area. In this view the coastal state would hold the residuum of powers in the economic zone and would be authorized to promulgate regulations with respect to pollution, scientific research, and even navigation. An early expression of the underdeveloped nations' concept of the economic zone appeared in the "Declaration of Santo Domingo," which emanated from a specialized conference of Caribbean countries on problems of the sea. That declaration contained the following paragraphs on the economic zone:

1. The coastal State has sovereign rights over the renewable and non-renewable resources, which are found in the waters, in the seabed and in the subsoil of an area adjacent to the territorial sea called the patrimonial sea.
2. The coastal State has the duty to promote and the right to regulate the conduct of scientific research within the patrimonial sea, as well as the right to adopt the necessary measures to prevent marine pollution and to ensure its sovereignty over the resources of the area.
3. The breadth of this zone should be the subject of an international agreement, preferably of a worldwide scope. The whole of the area of both the territorial sea and the patrimonial sea, taking into account geographic circumstances, should not exceed a maximum of 200 nautical miles . . . .
5. In this zone ships and aircraft of all States, whether coastal or not, should enjoy the right of freedom of navigation and overflight with no restrictions other than those resulting from the exercise by the coastal State of its rights within the area . . . .[5]

At the 1974 Caracas session of the Third Conference, Nicaragua introduced draft articles on the economic zone which can fairly be said to typify the interpretation of most underdeveloped nations. That proposal provided that:

The coastal State shall be entitled to a sea area adjacent to its coasts, up to a distance of 200 nautical miles measured from the applicable baseline. This area shall constitute the national sea of the coastal State. The delimitation of the national seas of adjacent or opposite coastal States shall be determined in accordance with the provisions of this Convention.

It shall be within the competence of the coastal State to make provision in its national sea for sovereign, jurisdictional or special powers, or combinations thereof with no limitations other than those provided for in this Convention.

The same right shall extend to the air space above the national sea, and to the submarine shelf which continues the territory of the State as far as the outer edge of the continental emersion. When the shelf does not extend as far as the outer limit of the national sea, the right of the coastal State shall extend to the sea-bed and the subsoil thereof as far as such outer limit.

The national sea, superjacent air space, submarine shelf and/or sea-bed and subsoil referred to in the preceding paragraph shall constitute the national zone of the coastal State, the integrity and inviolability of which shall be guaranteed by the international community.

Within the first 12 nautical miles of the national sea, beginning from the baseline drawn for such sea, the coastal State shall guarantee to foreign ships the right of innocent passage in accordance with the terms defined in this Convention.

In the national zone beyond the first 12 nautical miles referred to in the preceding paragraph, the coastal State shall guarantee to natural or juridical persons of third States that fishing, freedom of navigation, overflight, the laying of submarine cables and pipelines, and other legitimate uses of the zone shall be subject to no restrictions other than those provided for in this Convention and in treaties concluded subsequent thereto.[6]

Such interpretations are, of course, an anathema to naval powers and to industrialized nations heavily dependent on seaborne commerce for the maintenance of their economy.

Insofar as *fisheries* were concerned, the primary distinguishing characteristic between most of the proposals sponsored by the underdeveloped countries and those of the industrialized nations was the dichotomy between preferential and exclusive rights. The underdeveloped countries by and large sought *exclusive* jurisdiction over fisheries within their economic zone in order to exclude foreign fishing totally if they so chose. The developed nations, in turn, generally supported the concept of *preferential* rights that would require admission of foreign fishing effort in situations where the coastal state was incapable of harvesting the allowable catch of a particular stock. Although developed nations often argued that a preferential system would be the only way to ensure full utilization of living marine resources, the primary impetus for the argument—at least in the United States—came from the Department of Defense which although having to concede to a zonal approach on fishing jurisdiction, sought to restrict as much as possible the degree of coastal state discretion exercisable in the zone. Thus, in Caracas, the United States proposed a "full utilization" fisheries regime which contained the following language:

The coastal State shall ensure the full utilization of renewable resources within the economic zone.

For this purpose, the costal State shall permit nationals of other States to fish for that portion of the allowable catch of the renewable resources not fully utilized by its nationals, subject to the conservation measures adopted pursuant to article 12, and on the basis of the following priorities:

(a) States that have normally fished for a resource . . . .

(b) States in the region, particularly land-locked States and States with limited access to living resources off their coast; and

(c) all other States.

The coastal State may establish reasonable regulations and require the payment of reasonable fees for this purpose.[7]

At the same time that the economic zone debates were going on, the question of special treatment for anadromous species was taken up. The case for a separate legal regime for such species was forcefully articulated in a Canadian working paper submitted to the Conference, excerpts from which follow:

Salmon are unique in returning from the sea to the same fresh waters where they were born, to spawn and leave their fertilized eggs to develop in the same gravel beds. Following hatching, some salmon migrate directly to the sea as small fry; other species must live for one to several years in fresh water lakes or streams.

While salmon grow and mature in the open sea, they occupy the upper layers of cold northern waters where they are *not serious competitors* for the food supply of other valuable species. In the open sea they are found mainly in areas within the proposed 200-mile economic zones, but also, to a considerable degree, in areas beyond national jurisdiction.

Salmon are the only fish occurring in the open sea which man can and does increase by positive cultural measures. Such measures can be taken only by the State of origin.

Mixed in distant waters, salmon runs separate to return unerringly to their home streams. In distant waters salmon runs which need special protection are mixed with runs which are abundant; only as they approach their home streams (the very streams where they were bred) can the salmon runs be cropped separately and in accordance with the catches each run can support.

Salmon reach their greatest weight as they approach their home streams. During their migrations from the open sea to the spawning grounds, salmon grow faster than they die off. The greatest yield can be obtained by fishing the runs close to their home streams.

Strict regulations are needed to let the right number of spawners through the fisher to the spawning streams. This must be done by assessments of the runs as they appear, and prompt and often drastic restriction of fishing to let the optimum spawning run through. This requires costly supervision and enforcement, as well as co-operation of the fishermen. Only the State of origin of the salmon can carry out this essential function.[8]

Because few states have significant interests in anadromous species such as salmon, proposals such as that of Canada generated little enthusiasm. Japan, which fishes extensively for salmon on the high seas, opposed complete host state management and argued that freedom of fishing on the high seas should appertain both within and beyond the seaward boundary of any economic zone. A compromise proposal submitted by Denmark (whose interest in anadromous species stems from its Greenland fisheries) provided that:

The exploitation of anadromous species shall be regulated by agreement among interested States or by international arrangements through the appropriate intergovernmental fisheries organization.
    All interested States shall have an equal right to participate in such arrangements and organizations. Any arrangement shall take into account the interest of the State of origin and the interests of other coastal States.[9]

Even Japan, seeing the trend in the negotiations, offered a proposal at Caracas as follows:

The conservation and management of anadromous species shall be regulated through arrangements among the States participating in the exploitation of such species and, where appropriate, through regional intergovernmental organizations established for this purpose.
    The special interest of the coastal State, in whose fresh or estuarine waters anadromous species spawn, shall be taken into account in the arrangements for regulating such species.[10]

With virtually all fishery proposals in, the Conference adjourned to Geneva in its 1975 session.

The Revised Single Negotiating Text

At the conclusion of the 1975 Conference session in Geneva, the chairmen of the three main committees of the Conference each produced a "negotiating text" that he believed fairly reflected the consensus of the nations negotiating up to that time. Although one of these texts, and portions of the two others, were clearly not consensus in nature, most of the provisions concerning fisheries management did reflect a general sense of agreement on the part of those nations participating. Following the Spring 1976, session of the Conference in New York City further refinements were made on these negotiating texts, which were reissued under the heading "Revised Single Negotiating Text" (RSNT).[11] It will be useful to summarize the provisions of the RSNT on fisheries, since this will afford a glimpse of the future, whether the RSNT is ultimately adopted as a treaty or simply forms the basis of state action leading to the development of a rule of customary international law at some future date. (The full text of the articles of Part II of the RSNT dealing with fisheries are set forth in Annex C.)
    Article 44 would establish the "exclusive economic zone" extending up to 200 miles from the baseline, in which coastal states would have, *inter alia:*

Sovereign rights for the purpose of exploring and exploiting, conserving and managing the natural resources, whether living or non-living, of the bed and subsoil and the superjacent waters; . . .

Costal states are obligated to ensure that fisheries in their zone are not endangered by overexploitation and have authority to determine the allowable catch for stocks located within the zone. The management standard incorporated in the RSNT is "to maintain or restore populations of harvested species at levels at which can produce the maximum sustainable yield, as qualified by relevant environmental and economic factors, including the economic needs of coastal countries" [Art. 50 (3)]. In addition to traditional management objectives, the coastal state has the following obligation:

In establishing such measures the coastal State shall take into consideration the effects on species associated with or dependent upon harvested species with a view to maintaining or restoring populations of such associated or dependent species above levels at which their reproduction may become seriously threatened. Art. 50 (4).

The provisions of the RSNT on the utilization of living resources within the zone require the coastal state to promote the objective of optimum utilization of such resources in conformity with the management obligations already noted. The coastal state is obligated to enter into agreements or other arrangements to give other states access to any surplus of allowable catch that it does not have the capacity to harvest itself. However, since the coastal state has exclusive authority to determine its capacity to harvest living resources, this preferential character for the economic zone is largely illusory. In determining which states shall be allocated rights where the coastal state's capacity is below the allowable catch, the following factors are to be taken into consideration:

1. The significance of the renewable resources of the area to the economy of the coastal state concerned and its other national interest [Art. 51 (3)];

2. The right of landlocked states to participate in the exploitation of living resources of the zone on an equitable basis (Art. 58) and the rights of developing coastal states in a subregion or region whose geographical peculiarities makes such states particularly dependent for the satisfaction and nutritional needs of their populations upon the exploitation of the living resources in the zone of their neighboring states, as well as developing coastal states which can claim no exclusive economic zones of their own (Art. 59); and

3. The need to minimize economic dislocation in states whose nationals have habitually fished in the zone or which have made substantial efforts in research and identification of stocks [Art. 51 (3)].

The inclusion of traditional distant-water fishing nations within the criteria to be considered is again largely illusory in view of the preferences given to states in the region and the coastal state's right to consider the significance of fisheries to its economy and "its other national interests," the latter conceivably being subject to an interpretation of interests external to the fishery that would include politically motivated decisions.

The RSNT also provides that where stocks occur in the zones of two or more states, the states are obligated to seek through direct negotiations or regional organizations agreement on measures necessary to coordinate and ensure the conservation and development of such stocks (Art. 52). With respect to highly migratory species, both the coastal state and distant-water states are obligated to cooperate either through direct negotiation or through international organizations in order to ensure proper conservation and optimum utilization of such species both within and without the economic zone of the coastal state (Art. 53).

The RSNT provides with respect to anadromous stocks that the host state shall have the "primary interest in and responsibility for such stocks." Fishing for anadromous species is limited to the waters within the economic zone except in cases where such restrictions result in economic dislocation for a state other than the state of origin (Art. 55).

Clearly, then, the trend of the law of the sea negotiations is toward acceptance of an exclusive fishing zone in which the coastal state has exclusive management rights with respect to fisheries located there but which also has obligations to negotiate reasonable arrangements where stocks of fish either migrate in the zones of two or more countries or where the fisheries stock in question is highly migratory and thus found both within the zone and without. If this is in fact the trend, it can be argued that there is essentially no difference between the outcome envisioned through the law of the sea negotiations in the form of a treaty, on the one hand, and the outcome that would result from the unilateral assertion of 200-mile exclusive fishing zones by coastal nations, on the other hand. There are, however, a number of provisions of the RSNT that modify, however slightly, the unilateral proclamations of states that would probably not be included in those unilateral declarations. Among these are the specific duties relating to conservation and management, extending the concept of optimum sustainable yield to include economic and environmental factors and effects on associated or dependent species; the obligation, though largely illusory as mentioned, to admit distant-water fishing effort where the allowable catch is not harvested by the coastal state; the obligation to negotiate special arrangements with respect to highly migratory species; and the specification of preferences for landlocked states or developing states of the region in allocating access rights to foreign fishermen. It can be argued that most of these obligations are either illusory, or obligations only to negotiate, thus ensuring no particular outcome, and that such a situation offers little more than would be available for states in negotiating with a coastal nation that had unilaterally proclaimed an exclusive fishing zone.

The principal argument made in favor of a treaty agreement rather than law

development on a state practice basis is by the military establishments of the
United States, the Soviet Union, and some other industrially developed nations.
Their argument is based on the concept of "creeping jurisdiction," which posits
that coastal nations, if unrestrained by international agreement or law, tend to
assert an increasing range of competences over adjacent maritime areas to the
point where those competences become essentially a territorial sea. Territorial
seas of 200 miles throughout the world ocean pose very serious potential problems to naval mobility since vessels navigating within the territorial sea are subject to the rules of innocent passage, and because submarines transiting the
territorial waters must surface and show their flag. Thus, the United States
and other industrially advanced countries have pressed hard for a treaty solution
rather than a unilateral approach, though in the end the pressures brought on
the United States Congress by coastal fishermen in the United States resulted
in that nation establishing a 200-mile exclusive fisheries management zone before many underdeveloped countries did so.

The Role of the International Court of Justice

As noted in the last chapter, the "cod war" between Iceland and the United
Kingdom and other European nations reached a new peak of intensity with
Iceland's move from a 12-mile to a 50-mile exlcusive fishing zone. The United
Kingdom sought to invoke the jurisdiction of the International Court of Justice
in the case, and although Iceland steadfastly refused to appear before the Court
on the grounds that it had no jurisdiction over the dispute, the Court nonetheless took the matter under advisement and in 1973 issued temporary injunctions
concerning the amount of fish to be taken from within Iceland's claimed zone
pending the Court's decision on the merits of the case. Most observers expected
that the Court would defer handing down its substantive decision until after the
conclusion of the law of the sea conference in Caracas in the summer of 1974.
To the surprise of almost everyone, however, the Court announced its decision
virtually in the middle of the Caracas session.

The Court held that Iceland's claim of an exclusive fishery zone was "not
opposable" to the United Kingdom and to the Federal Republic of Germany,
but went beyond that limited holding to recognize both preferential rights for
Iceland and established rights for the distant-water fishing nations in stocks of
fish more than 12 miles from Iceland's coast, concluding its decision with a
mandate to the parties involved to negotiate an equitable settlement.[12] Although some of the fine points of the Court's decision are interesting and will
be elaborated on shortly, it must be observed at the outset that the International
Court of Justice has virtually no impact on international affairs. The Court
handles very few cases and those seldom involve matters of critical importance
simply because the jursdiction of the Court is consensual in nature, and no

nation is likely to submit a matter critical to its national security on such a voluntary basis. Further, there is no enforcement agency to carry out the orders of the Court, enforcement being a matter of voluntary compliance. When one compares the International Court of Justice to, for example, the Supreme Court of the United States, the differences are even more clearly marked. The United States Supreme Court has the weight of the Executive Branch for enforcement of its decisions and decrees, and because of early decisions and longstanding practices has had a far-reaching impact on the social, economic, and political fabric of the United States. The world court, by comparison, has had virtually no impact on international social, economic, or political affairs, hears few cases, and is completely without power to enforce its decisions.

Its status notwithstanding, the comments of the Court are interesting simply because they reflect the views of learned international legal scholars on certain aspects of the law of the sea relating to high seas fisheries management. The Court made a number of pronouncements and observations, several of which are important in the sense that they probably reflect the directions or likely future directions of state practice or agreement through the Third Conference.

First, the Court concluded that exclusive fishing zones extending no more than 12 miles from the coast were internationally valid as a matter of customary international law. Few would have disputed the contention that such zones were valid at least to twelve miles and although the statement by the Court is purely dicta (that issue not being before it in the "cod war" dispute) it is nevertheless one more bit of evidence leading to the conclusion that 12-mile exclusive fishing zones are permissable as a matter of customary state practice and "law."

Second, the Court held that as a matter of customary international law coastal states are entitled to "preferential" rights in fishery stocks off their coasts in situations where (1) there is a special dependence of the coastal state on fishery resources, and (2) there is a need to limit catch in a given fishery to a level below that currently taken by all states fishing in the area. Such rights, according to the Court, are to be implemented by agreement between the states concerned. The Court drew on a number of sources in reaching its conclusion, relying heavily on the deliberations of the First and Second UN Conferences on the Law of the Sea held in 1958 and 1960, respectively. However, the Court has been severely criticized on this point for reaching its conclusion without adequate evidence.[13] The situation of Iceland is, in fact, fairly unique because Iceland is not only heavily dependent on its coastal fishery for economic viability, but it is dependent to a degree unmatched by any other nation. The assertion in the specific case before the Court that Iceland's heavy dependence on its coastal fishery for its economic livelihood entitled it to some preferential treatment vis-a-vis distant-water fishing nations exercising the right of freedom of high seas fishing could easily be justified. For example, the "reasonableness" requirement of Article 2 of the Convention on the High Seas could be invoked to support the argument that distant-water fishing fleets that took fish in such a manner as to rend the economic fabric of the coastal state did so without reasonable regard to the interests of that coastal state in fishing those same stocks. To generalize, however, and to assert that on a global basis coastal states have preferential rights in fisheries beyond the 12-mile zone is difficult to justify from state practice or the traditional methods of determining the existence of a rule of customary international law. Clearly, the direction of the Third Conference appears to be taking it beyond the holding of the Court since the outcome of the Conference, assuming it produces any agreement, is likely to be the validation of exclusive rather than preferential economic zones. The Court, however, is bound to apply the law as it finds it, and it is certainly questionable whether the finding of preferential rights as a matter of customary international law is justified by the evidence.

Third, the Court offset its preferential rights finding by recognizing the rights of states other than coastal states that have traditionally fished in the area. The Court noted that "considerations similar to those which prompted the recognition of the preferential rights of the coastal state in a special situation apply when coastal populations and other fishing states are also dependent on certain fishing grounds." Certainly under existing international law, foreign nations have the right to engage in the high seas freedom of fishing more than 12 miles from a coastal state. The Court went beyond this holding, however, in ascribing a special status for those nations that had traditionally fished in an area and that were dependent on it vis-a-vis those states that had not done so and that would have to rely simply on a high seas freedom of fishing to engage in exploitation of stocks in the area. Again, it is difficult to find in the evidence discussed in the Court's opinion a justification for establishing a preference among non-coastal states in the exercise of their rights of high seas freedom of fishing. Nonetheless, in the context of the Iceland–United Kingdom dispute, it certainly makes sense to discuss the equities involved with the nations before the Court, and the ICJ cannot be faulted for attempting to achieve some equitable balance. However, as a general international legal principle, the idea of established rights seems to lack foundation in the evidence.

Fourth, and finally, the Court noted that its newly defined concepts of preferential and established rights were not static and that both the degree of dependence and the status of fishery stocks might change over time. Most importantly, the Court stated that:

[T]he former laissez faire treatment of the living resources of the sea in the high seas has been replaced by recognition of a duty to have due regard to the rights of other states and the needs of conservation for the benefit of all.

Clearly the Court here is on firm ground. All the evidence points to the fact that the open access, freedom of the high seas regime is detrimental to both the fish and the fishing industry. The Court's proposed solution, although perhaps useful in the particular situation before the Court, does not appear to be the type of measure suited to the resolution of the international fisheries management problem. Indeed, it is even questionable whether the Court's pronouncement was of any assistance in resolving the dispute, since not long after the decision Iceland extended its exclusive fishing zone from 50 to 200 miles thereby setting off another round in the "cod war" that proved to be the most heated of all the segments in this 20-year conflict.

In the end, Iceland prevailed. In November 1975, the Federal Republic of Germany and the Netherlands entered into agreements implicitly recognizing Iceland's 200-mile fishing zone and accepting severe limitations on their rights of access and catch within that zone. Then, in June 1976, the British capitulated and signed a similar agreement by which their access and catches were restricted within the zone. Quite clearly, then, the trend evidenced by state practice is not that asserted by the International Court of Justice as new rules of customary international law. Neither does the trend appear to be the "preferential" rights system envisioned in the current RSNT produced by the law of the sea conference. Rather, the future appears to lie in unilaterally promulgated exclusive fishing zones.

The most comprehensive legislation establishing such a zone was signed into law by the President of the United States on April 13, 1976. The next chapter is devoted to an analysis of that legislation in view of its obvious portents for the future of international fisheries management. Before turning to that law, however, some attention must be directed to a general assessment of the likely future development of the international law of fisheries and to some of the probable results of that development.

Likely Future Developments in International Fisheries Management[14]

It has been clear for several years that an integral part of any law of the sea agreement must be the recognition of broad coastal state jurisdiction over living marine resources, probably to a distance of 200 miles from the coast. State practice and express declarations make it clear that virtually all coastal nations will extend their fishery jurisdiction to 200 miles from their coasts if no agreement is produced to that effect in the Conference. Some dozen underdeveloped nations already have claimed 200-mile fishing zones, and such responsible members of the international community as Mexico, Norway, Iceland, Canada, and the United States are on the verge of or have already adopted such limits. It is equally clear that unilaterally proclaimed zones would, for the most part, be exclusive in nature, i.e., without any legal obligation to admit foreign fishing. Whether in fact all foreign fishing would be totally excluded in such zones is problematic, although consequences of such action will be briefly discussed in this section.

It should be noted that even if a large number of 200-mile exclusive fishing zone claims were to be made, practice under such claims would have to continue for a period of time sufficient to constitute "usage" for purposes of forming customary international law. The claims would not in themselves *ipso facto* create customary international law.

The most likely outcome of the Conference appears to be the establishment of broad *exclusive* fishing zones, so that the consequences of nonagreement would not be significantly different for fisheries than the consequences of agreement, at least insofar as the type of jurisdiction over living resources that is being claimed. What is important to consider, then, are the likely general consequences of the unilateral establishment of broad fishing zones (including the case of preferential zones since some nations will, even though acting unilaterally, honor during a transitional period certain historic rights of distant-water fishing nations).

Exclusive Fishing Zone Claims: Responses

There are four principal categories of responses by distant-water fishing states to the unilateral establishment of broad, exclusive fishing zones in areas where such foreign nations have fished or wish to fish.

Abandonment; Displacement. First, the distant-water nations might abandon any attempt to fish in such zones. This could result in some economic dislocation where the abstaining state had previously fished in the area, the quantity of adverse effects depending on (1) the amount of fishing undertaken there, and (2) the opportunities for displacement to other resources.

Second, displacement could simply shift the conflict from one set of adversary nations to another set without actually reducing the difficulties. Given the investment in distant-water fishing gear of the major distant-water fishing nations, this seems a likely outcome, meaning that the conflict would ultimately surface somewhere.

Third, and most beneficially, displacement might occur, but to previously unutilized high seas species of living marine resources. This would have the dual benefit of avoiding a coastal state–distant-water state conflict, and developing new sources of protein.

Negotiated Access. Access arrangements could be negotiated between the zonal state and the distant-water fishing state (or between the business entities involved). The United States–Brazil shrimp agreement is an example of the former, and the joint ventures being negotiated between Japanese fishing companies and several coastal nations constitute an example of the latter. A recent example of negotiated access concerns the Mexican 200-mile exclusive zone. Mexico enacted its 200-mile fishing zone bill in February 1976, giving public notice that it would take effect 120 days following its publication in the Mexican federal register. The original date of implementation for the law was June 6, 1976. This action alarmed United States shrimp fishermen operating from the Texas coast, who regularly fished in the Campeche Bank area off the Yucatan peninsula and in other areas off the coast of Mexico. Rather than engage in confrontation, however, the United States Government sent a fishery delegation to Mexico. Those negotiations were in progress at the time the Mexican law was to have entered into force. Recognizing that fact, Mexico postponed application of the new measure until July 31 to provide time for negotiation of a fishing treaty. That treaty was successfully negotiated, and the Mexican law entered into force on August 1. Though there is dissatisfaction among United States shrimping interests with the phase-out provisions of the treaty, the approach taken by the two nations indicates a likely procedure for use in similar fishing zone claim situations.

Because government-to-government agreements might involve matter extraneous to the fishery, which, given a change in circumstances, could adversely affect the stability of such arrangements, it seems possible that business arrangements—perhaps including economic development incentives by the distant-water fishermen in the nature of construction of processing plants and the like—will be the more favored route. Indeed, the Soviet Union is already said to be negotiating with American firms for joint venture fishing arrangements in preparation for the enforcement of fishing zone legislation by the United States Congress (one such agreement, between Sovrybflot and Bellingham Cold Storage, has already been executed). That such agreements can be reached and conflict avoided, even in cases of intense disagreement, was demonstrated by the recent action of Canada in barring Soviet fishing vessels from its ports for alleged violations of the quota system of the International Convention for Northwest Atlantic Fisheries. This unilateral action by Canada precipitated diplomatic talks that resulted in action sufficiently satisfactory to the Canadians to warrant their reopening ports to the Soviet vessels. This sort of accommodation is likely to be repeated many times in the case of unilaterally established 200-mile fishing zones.

Legal Conflict. The distant-water state could (although the previous alternative will probably predominate in most cases) refuse to recognize the legal validity of such extended zones. The resultant conflict could take one of two directions: (1) resolution by peaceful means, perhaps through adjudication in the International Court of Justice (bilateral settlement would be more akin to the second option, above, in which governments negotiate access treaties) or (2) physical conflict, initiated by the distant-water nation's use of military support for its claimed high seas fishing freedom or by the seizure of vessels by the coastal state. If past precedent is any guide, such conflicts are usually isolated and, although contributing to poor relations between the countries involved, do not result in extended hostilities. Rather, when the interests involved are perceived by the actors to be of such value as to warrant the threat or use of force, a new appreciation of the situation occurs leading to new attempts at peaceful settlement of disputes. For example, in spite of continued reoccurrences of conflict in the "cod war" since the later 1950s, each crisis has resulted in a new settlement that accommodated the interests of the parties involved for some period of time. However, such conflicts are inevitable in a period of law change whether that change occurs by treaty or customary processes, and history demonstrates that this type of conflict is more likely to lead to ultimate peaceful settlement than to any general outbreak of hostilities.

Economic Retaliation. Finally, distant-water states might reject the legality of such zonal claims, but, rather than contesting the issue in the fishing arena, take measures against the coastal state in other economic areas. For example, the distant-water nation could impose economic sanctions against the coastal state in the nature of suspension of aid (if the relation were developed to underdeveloped nation), or it could boycott exports of raw materials (in the case of an underdeveloped to developed nation relationship). A good example of such a situation involving two developed nations would be the United States and Japan, should the former attempt to exclude Japanese fishing effort from its unilaterally proclaimed 200-mile zone. If Japan refused to recognize the validity of such a zone, it is likely that she would advise her nationals to continue to fish within the zone on the basis that the area constituted high seas. It is even possible that Japan would enact the equivalent of the U.S. Fishermen's Protective Act providing for reimbursement of fines paid by Japanese fishermen as a result of United States enforcement of the 200-mile fishery zone. Although such an outcome is conceivable, present indications point to a much more amicable settlement, primarily through the negotiation of business arrangements between Japanese and United States fishing concerns.

All the possibilities noted above would apply equally to the situations where (1) the coastal state claimed only a preferential zone (except that the challenge of legal validity would probably not occur because of the recognition of the legal right of the distant-water state to fish within the zone; the dispute would, rather, then be over the amount of allowable catch), and (2) jurisdiction over anadromous species throughout their migratory range is claimed by the host state.

It would appear that a great deal of diplomatic disturbance, and perhaps even an occasional incident of violence, could be avoided by the sucessful completion of a treaty on fishing rights. If *all* nations acceded to the principle of an exclusive 200-mile fishing zone, then either the agreement would contain features satisfactory to distant-water fishing nations or such nations would have concluded that their interests could be fairly well served through bilateral arrangements. Since the former seems an unlikely occurrence, the situation of agreement differs little from that of nonagreement. The principal consequence of nonagreement on fisheries is that distant-water fishing nations will have to rely on bilateral negotiations for access to present fishing grounds within 200 miles of another nation's coast, but the situation is really about the same as with an exclusive zone treaty provision. Even the recognition of preferential rights in a treaty would not remove negotiating problems entirely, for there would still be the questions of compliance with the treaty definition of traditional rights, priorities among competing traditional fishing nations, the amount of allowable catch, and conditions of access. Conflicts, even violent ones, could just as easily arise over an exclusion pursuant to treaty interpretation as pursuant to unilateral action. As a result, it seems fair to conclude—if one accepts the proposition that the treaty outcome would be legitimization of 200-mile exclusive or preferential fishing zones—that the consequences of nonagreement would differ little from the consequences of agreement insofar as conflicts over access to fishing grounds are concerned. A possible exception to this comment exists with respect to salmon on the high seas, where coastal states may not be willing to accept the costs of enforcement at great distances from the coast. In this case, high seas fishing for salmon by states other than the host state would continue, requiring bilateral or multilateral solution in the absence of an overall treaty.

Consequences for Existing Arrangements

Unilaterally established 200-mile exclusive fishing zones will obviously introduce a conflict between the proclaiming state and existing international fishery commissions and conventions. If 200-mile economic zones are established by international agreement, account can be taken of existing commissions and conventions, and their role can be defined in relationship to the new jurisdictional arrangements. If, however, 200-mile zones are created on a unilateral basis, they may not accommodate existing commissions and conventions, since, presumably, it is at least in part the failure of existing arrangements to adequately manage high seas fisheries that will have resulted in the unilateral claims.

There are two principal effects of such a conflict. First, there could be a disruption of the useful work of existing fishery commissions and, possibly, a dissolution of some of those commissions, resulting in a loss of data on which management judgements are based. Second, vessels operating under color of law through existing conventions may be more prone to contest the proclamation of unilateral jurisdiction than if the area were unregulated high seas. This may, therefore, result in conflicts where the nations representing the vessels and the nation having proclaimed the 200-mile zone each believe that they have a valid legal basis for their actions.

Notes

1. Some of the material in this section originally appeared in a paper entitled "Legal Aspects of Sea Power" prepared for a dialog at the Woodrow Wilson International Center for Scholars (February 1975). It is reproduced here, in revised form, with permission of the Woodrow Wilson International Center for Scholars.

2. For other documents covering the early phases of the law of the sea negotiations, see H. Gary Knight (ed.), *The Law of the Sea: Cases, Documents, and Readings* (Washington, D.C.: Nautilus Press, 1976-1977 edition), p. 545 *et seq.*

3. See United States Revised Draft Fisheries Article, UN Doc. A/AC. 138/SC.II/L.9 (4 August 1972).

4. Proposals for a Regime of Fisheries on the High Seas: Submitted by Japan, UN Doc. A/AC.138/SC.II/L.12 (14 August 1972); The Union of Soviet Socialist Republics: Draft Article on Fishing, UN Doc. A/AC.138/SC.II/L.6 (18 July 1972).

5. Declaration of Santo Domingo, Specialized Conference of the Caribbean Countries on Problems of the Sea, June 7, 1972, UN Doc. A/AC.138/80 (26 July 1972).

6. Working Document Submitted by Nicaragua—National Zone: Characteristics, UN Doc. A/CONF.62/C.2/L.17 (23 July 1974).

7. United States of America: Draft Articles for a Chapter on the Economic Zone and the Continental Shelf, UN Doc. A/CONF.62/C.2/L.47 (8 August 1974), part II, art. 13.

8. Working Paper Submitted by the Delegation of Canada, UN Doc. A/CONF.62/C.2/L.81 (23 August 1974).

9. Denmark: Draft Article on Anadromous Species, UN Doc. A/CONF. 62/C.2/L.37 (5 August 1974).

10. Japan: Draft Article on Anadromous Species, UN Doc. A/CONF. 62/C.2/L.46 (8 August 1974).

11. Revised Single Negotiating Text, UN Doc. No. A/CONF.62/WP.8/Rev. 1/parts I, II, and III (6 May 1976) and A/CONF.62/WP.9/Rev. 1 (6 May 1976).

12. Fisheries Jurisdiction case (Merits), (1974) I.C.J. 3, 175.

13. See Churchill, "The Fisheries Jurisdiction Cases: The Contribution of the International Court of Justice to the Debate on Coastal States' Fisheries Rights," *International and Comparative Law Quarterly* 24 (1975): 82-105.

14. Some material in this section was originally published in H. Gary Knight, "Consequences of Non-Agreement at the Third U.N. Law of the Sea Conference," © 1976 by the American Society of International Law. It is reproduced here, in revised form, with permission of the American Society of International Law.

6

The United States "Fishery Conservation and Management Act of 1976"

Before discussing the substance of the United States 200-mile exclusive fishery management legislation, a brief overview of the structure of the various fishing industries in the United States and of the evolution of National fisheries policy will be presented. Only against this background can many of the provisions of the "Fishery Conservation and Management Act of 1976" (FCMA) be clearly understood.

United States Fisheries Policy Prior to 1976[1]

Modern United States high seas fishery policy began with the "second" Truman Proclamation of 1945.[2] As noted in Chapter 4, that document stated that the United States government regarded as proper the establishment of "explicitly bounded" conservation zones in high seas areas but that where fishing activities there involved the nationals of other countries such zones were to be established only pursuant to agreements between the United States and the other affected states (similar rights were recognized for other nations, provided the interests of the United States fishermen operating off their coasts were similarly recognized). This policy was entirely consistent with the obligations later assumed by the United States when it became a party to the Convention on Fishing and Conservation of the Living Resources of the High Seas. Although the United States put forward more sophisticated proposals during the current law of the sea negotiations, the Truman Proclamation remained the cornerstone of United States high seas fishing policy until 1976, with one modification in 1966. The fundamental bases of that policy are that (1) areas more than 3 miles from the coast constitute high seas and are therefore subject to freedom of fishing as one of the recognized freedoms of the high seas, (2) management and conservation systems on the high seas are proper only if they are the product of agreement among all affected nations, and (3) no nation has the right to unilaterally exclude other nations from fishing beyond the 3-mile limit.

In 1954, in response to tuna boat seizures by Latin American nations, the United States adopted the Fishermen's Protective Act, which, as noted in Chapter 4, provided for reimbursement of fines levied against vessels seized in areas that the United States Government did not recognize as being subject to the exclusive fisheries jurisdiction of the coastal state in question.[3]

In 1966, the United States adopted a 12-mile exclusive fishing zone. The Exclusive Fisheries Zone Act of 1966 established a fisheries zone contiguous to the territorial sea of the United States in which the nation "exercises the same exclusive rights in respect to fisheries . . . as it has in its territorial sea."[4] Fishing within the 12-mile zone without United States permission was made a criminal offense by the Bartlett Act.[5] As will be noted later in this chapter, both the 12-mile Exclusive Fisheries Zone Act and the Bartlett Act were repealed by the Fishery Conservation and Management Act of 1976.

Considering the trend of the law of the sea negotiations toward ever broader fishery zones, it is not likely that any future domestic or international developments will restrictively affect the 12-mile zone. The importance of the 1966 legislation for future fisheries policy, however, is that the United States did not automatically terminate all foreign fishing in the zone, when it was promulgated. The first section of the Act provides that the claimed exclusive fishing rights are "subject to the continuation of traditional fishing by foreign states within this zone as may be recognized by the United States." The United States subsequently recognized traditional fishing rights in agreements with Canada[6] and Mexico.[7] Other agreements, providing access to the zone but without recognizing traditional rights *per se,* were negotiated with Japan, Poland, Romania, South Korea, and the Soviet Union.[8]

Pursuant to the Convention on the Continental Shelf, the United States is possessed of exclusive rights with respect to sedentary species of living marine resources located on its continental shelf.

The Bartlett Act implements United States rights under the Continental Shelf Convention by making it unlawful (subject to limited exceptions by executive agreement provided under the Bartlett Act) for foreign fishing crews to take resources of the shelf appertaining to the United States. Species falling within the sedentary classification, as determined by the United States, are specified in a rider to the "Offshore Shrimp Fisheries Act of 1973."[9]

Effective December 5, 1974, the United States government adopted a new policy with respect to continental shelf fishery resources, providing for the arrest and seizure of vessels taking such resources (except as provided in bilateral agreements) in cases where either fishing on the high seas involved gear designed specifically to catch continental shelf fishery resources, or high seas fishing could be expected to result in the catch of continental shelf fishery resources.[10]

This, then, was the status of United States fishery policy and law prior to 1976. These laws and regulations, as well as the 1976 Act, were responsive to the needs and interests of various segments of the United States fishing industry. Those interests are outlined in the next section.

United States Fishery Interests

The fishing industry in the United States can be classified in five categories—tuna, coastal, salmon (and other anadromous species), shrimp, and sedentary.

The *tuna* industry relies on highly sophisticated gear and operates primarily off the western coasts of the continents of South America and Africa. Although tuna are a highly migratory species of fish, a substantital portion of the fishing activity of the United States distant-water tuna fleet takes place within 200 miles of foreign coastlines. The tuna industry has, therefore, borne the brunt of the conflict of views between the United States, on the one hand, and Chile, Ecuador, and Peru on the other hand, concerning the international legal validity of 200-mile exclusive fishing zones. Vessels of the tuna fleet have been harassed, arrested, detained, and fired on when attempting to operate within the 200-mile limit adjacent to the so-called CEP countries that seek to impose a licensing requirement to validate the presence of vessels within such zones. Accordingly, the tuna industry would prefer, regardless of other arrangements emanating from the Conference, to maintain its right to follow the tuna wherever they may migrate, subject to international management arrangements, without additional economic burdens imposed by the existence of 200-mile economic resource zones. The tuna fishermen are the principal beneficiaries of the Fishermen's Protective Act.

The *coastal* fishing industry in the United States operates, by definition, off our own coasts. The United States coastal fishing industry has not fared particularly well in the face of competition from the distant-water fishing fleets of the Soviet Union, Japan, the United Kingdom, Germany, and other nations. Heavy fishing pressure, primarily from foreign fleets, has caused sharp declines in many of the stocks on which United States fishing crews rely for a living. The position of the industry has generally been one of securing unilateral legislation that would give the United States the right to exclude distant-water fleets from the United States coastal fishing areas (or to regulate them on admission) to permit recovery of the stocks, to provide a better opportunity for the United States fleet to exploit these resources, and to maintain the economic viability of the domestic fishing industry. Coastal fishermen wanted to see the Bartlett Act or its equivalent extended to a 200-mile zone off the coast of the United States.

The *anadromous* fishing industry (principally salmon, but including other species as well) is not in a position to rely exclusively either on a zonal approach (such as is generally desired by the coastal fishery in the United States) or on an open access regime. Although anadromous species spawn in the fresh and estuarine waters of the United States, they range far and wide on the high seas, well beyond 200 miles, and they are thus subject to harvest by distant-water fishing fleets when outside the limits of national jurisdiction. The anadromous fisheries industry therefore desires that the host state have an exclusive right to manage the catch of anadromous species. Their position is akin to that of the coastal fishermen who desire exclusive access to the resource but differs in that even a 200-mile economic resource zone would be insufficient in itself to secure the requisite species protection.

The *shrimp* industry in the United States has interests similar to both the coastal industry and the tuna industry. Most shrimp fishing is done off the coasts of the United States, principally in the Gulf of Mexico, but approximately 20 percent is conducted off the coasts of Mexico, Guyana, Brazil, and other foreign nations. Thus the shrimpers, although desiring the exclusive right to harvest shrimp resources off the coasts of the United States, do not wish at the same time to endanger their access to shrimp resources off the coasts of other states. The agreement between the United States and Brazil concerning access to shrimp resources within the latter's 200-mile fishing zone illustrates one solution to the problem faced by the shrimping industry in the face of the economic resource zone concept.

Finally, United States fishermen exploiting *sedentary* species of living marine organisms from the United States continental shelf (primarily lobster and crab) already have exclusive jurisdiction with respect to such species pursuant to the Convention on the Continental Shelf. No legal protection beyond the Bartlett Act, the Offshore Shrimp Fisheries Act of 1973, and the 1976 continental shelf regulations was sought by harvesters of continental shelf sedentary resources, although they could realize benefits by a reduction in the amount of high seas fishing effort where that effort has resulted in damage to their gear or in an incidental catch of sedentary species.

The "Fishery Conservation and Management Act of 1976"

Legislative History

The first serious attempt by Congress to enact a 200-mile exclusive fishing zone bill occurred during 1974. Hearings were held before a subcommittee of the House Committee on Merchant Marine and Fisheries from May to October 1974,[11] although the bills under consideration did not come to a floor vote in the House during 1974. In the Senate, three committees—Commerce, Foreign Relations, and Armed Services—were given jurisdiction over the 200-mile fishery zone bill introduced in that chamber (S. 1988), and hearings were held in all three committees during 1974.[12] All three committees filed reports on the proposed legislation[13] with Commerce and Armed Services reporting the bill favorably, Foreign Relations unfavorably. The bill, S. 1988, passed the Senate by a vote of 68–27 in December 1974. The House not having acted, however, the measure died with the conclusion of the 93d Congress.

Efforts were renewed in the 94th Congress during 1975, beginning with Hearings on H.R. 200 before a subcommittee of the House Committee on Merchant Marine and Fisheries during March 1975.[14] The House Committee on International Relations also made a special oversight report on the pending legislation.[15] On the Senate side, the Committees on Commerce, Foreign

Relations, and Armed Services once again shared jurisdiction, with the Senate Commerce Committee holding two hearings on S. 961, on June 6 and September 19, 1975,[16] the Senate Foreign Relations Committee holding a hearing on October 31, 1975,[17] and the Senate Armed Services Committee holding a hearing on November 19, 1975.[18] Each of the three committees filed a separate report[19] with the Foreign Relations Committee again constituting the sole adverse reaction.

H.R. 200 passed the House of Representatives on October 9, 1975, by a vote of 208-101, and S. 961 passed the Senate on January 28, 1976, by a vote of 77-19. A Committee of Conference was appointed to consider the two versions of the bill, and it filed its report on March 24, 1976.[20] The Senate approved the Conference Committee's compromise bill by voice vote on March 29, 1976, and the House also acted favorably, by a margin of 346-52 on March 30, 1976. The President of the United States signed the Act on April 13, 1976.[21] A complete legislative history of the Act, including the 1975 Committee reports and the House and Senate floor debates on the respective versions of the Act (H.R. 200 and S. 961), has been published by the U.S. government and is available from the Superintendent of Documents.[22]

Arguments Concerning 200-Mile Fisheries Zone Legislation

Principal Argument in Favor of Enactment. The principal argument in favor of the Act was that excessive fishing within 200 miles of the coast of the United States had depleted the available fishery resources to such an extent that the future economic utility of many species was in doubt. Among the stocks often mentioned in this category were haddock, herring, mackerel, manhaden, sable fish, shrimp, yellowtail flounder, halibut, pollack, yellowfin sole, and hake. Likewise there existed a danger to anadromous species, particularly salmon, from high seas harvesting, the argument being that the only biologically sound site for the harvesting of anadromous species was near the coast on their return to their streams of origin. Overfishing of all these stocks, the argument continued, was attributable in large measure to massive foreign fishing efforts, though this argument did not address the evidence that depletion of some of the coastal stocks might have been attributable to United States fishermen.

Proponents further argued that international fishery agreements to which the United States was a party and that purported to regulate and control fishing efforts on overfished stocks had been relatively ineffective in their objectives. Because of the unlikelihood of reaching timely agreement on a comprehensive and widely accepted law of the sea treaty that would almost certainly provide for 200-mile fishery zones, there existed a danger of further overfishing of other stocks. Therefore, the argument concluded, the United States, both in its own interest and in the interest of preserving threatened stocks of fish, must take immediate action to manage, regulate, and control both the taking of fish within 200 miles of its shore, and the taking of anadromous species of fish and continental shelf fishery resources beyond such limit, pending international agreement on an acceptable treaty.

Principal Arguments in Opposition to Enactment. Opponents of the Act noted that pursuant to both customary international law and the Convention on the High Seas, freedom of fishing was protected beyond the seaward limit of the territorial sea. To assert exclusive competence over such areas would therefore violate the well-established international principle of freedom of the high seas, at least insofar as fishing rights were concerned. Proponents argued that the present law was simply not all that clear—there being no agreement on the permissible limits of coastal states fishery jurisdiction—particularly in light of the opinions in the *Fisheries Jurisdiction Case.* The I.C.J. did not in that decision answer the specific question of the international legal validity of exclusive fishing zones beyond 12 miles from the coast, but it did specifically state that (at least for the nations involved in that dispute) the coastal state had some preferential rights to fishery resources beyond 12 miles. Enactment of domestic legislation could therefore be reasonably interpreted as a determination that the United States, as a coastal nation, had a "special dependence" on coastal fishery resources and a need to limit the catch of those resources. Further, Article 2 of the Convention on the High Seas states that freedom of fishing (*inter alia*) is to be undertaken "with reasonable regard to the interests of other States in their exercise of the freedom of the high seas." This indicated to some international lawyers that the freedom of fishing was not an absolute freedom but might be circumscribed in certain situations where the exercise of the freedom in unrestrained fashion would be unreasonable (e.g., where the effort would result in stock extinction).

Opponents of the Act pointed out that unilateral extensions of fishery jurisdiction have created conflicts in the past. The prime examples given were the "tuna war" between the United States and west coast Latin American nations, which arose from the latters' extension of 200-mile fishing zones in the late 1940s and early 1950s, and the "cod war" between Iceland and the United Kingdom, which was initiated by Iceland's move to a 12-mile fishing zone in 1958 and exacerbated by its claims of 50 miles in 1972 and 200 miles in 1975. The substance of the argument was that such unilateral actions impinge—or at least are perceived to impinge—on existing high seas freedoms of other nations, with a resultant confrontation between two nations or groups of nations each claiming mutually exclusive interests in the same resources. Nations with an established interest in world peace and stability, such as the United States, therefore had a vital interest in seeing matters such as fishery resource conflicts settled by peaceful negotiation rather than by unilateral legislative action.

Proponents of the Act pointed out that: (1) there is a trend toward international legitimization of 200-mile exclusive fishing zones and that, as was the case with the Truman Proclamation of 1945 concerning the continental shelf, unilateral action can actually speed up the process of the emergence of new norms of international law; (2) the instances of real violence and disruption of international relations over fishery conflicts were few in number and did not provide sufficient precedents from which to conclude that extension of fisheries jurisdiction by the United States would lead to open conflict; and (3) the Act provided for continuation, through permits, of fishing by foreign nations, the United States having demonstrated in the past a willingness to avoid abrupt economic dislocation for distant-water fishermen when it extended its fisheries zone from 3 to 12 miles in 1966 without incident or conflict.

The major argument advanced by the Department of State and other government representatives was that the measure would prejudice the success of the Law of the Sea Conference and thereby adversely affect other U.S. ocean interests. They suggested that unilateral claims of fishery jurisdiction had led to or encouraged more extreme claims and that such claims could have an adverse impact on a broad range of United States ocean interests, including commercial navigation and naval mobility. The Act, however, related solely to fishing jurisdiction and did not purport to expand or extend United States jurisdiction in any other regard and most particularly not with regard to regulation of navigation. Proponents of the Act pointed out that the dire contentions of cause and effect stemming from enactment were purely speculative and were generally unsupported by any direct evidence.

Opponents of the Act urged that the United States continue to rely, for an interim period at least, on bilateral agreements and international fishery commissions, such as the International Convention for Northwest Atlantic Fisheries (ICNAF), to regulate fishing activities off its coasts. The State Department, with the support of the President, had undertaken extensive efforts during 1975 to renegotiate bilateral treaties and to negotiate within ICNAF and other international fishery commissions for quotas and other conditions more favorable to United States interests. They pointed to alleged successes in multilateral fora, such as ICNAF, and to bilateral negotiations such as the 1975 agreements with Romania and Poland. These efforts, it was argued, should not be impaired by enacting unilateral legislation prior to conclusion of the Third United Nations Conference on the Law of the Sea.

Proponents pointed out that essentially the same negotiations would be undertaken—indeed, were required to be undertaken in the Act—if the United States were to extend its fishery jurisdiction to 200 miles. In that case, however, the United States would have much more bargaining leverage, since it would have the jurisdictional base from which to completely exclude foreign fishing (or domestic fishing for that matter) unless the fishermen agreed to comply with reasonable regulations. Further, it was observed that in spite of the recent negotiating efforts, some modestly successful, the track record of fishery management by international agreement was not good, and there was no reason to suspect that this approach could suddenly be transformed into an effective management device, although in fairness it should be observed that past domestic fishery management efforts have in large measure been equally ineffective.

It was also argued that unilateral extension of United States fisheries jurisdiction could seriously injure United States tuna and distant-water shrimp fishing crews, that operate within 200 miles of other nations. The reasoning was twofold: (1) United States action could encourage other nations not presently claiming extended fishing jurisdiction to enact their own 200-mile exclusive fishing zones, with resultant displacement of United States distant-water fishing effort now taking place on the high seas but within 200 miles of the coast; and (2) United States action could invalidate our protests to nations already claiming such zones and would render the Fishermen's Protective Act inapplicable to distant-water fishing in such areas.

Proponents of the Act pointed out that whether the United States acted or not, there was a clear trend toward establishment of 200-mile fishing zones and that this was also the likely outcome of the Third LOS Conference. Therefore, to withhold enactment would probably not affect the implementation of such zones by other states and, in fact, most of the nations off whose coasts United States shrimp and tuna fishermen presently operate had already claimed 200-mile fishing or territorial sea zones (Brazil, Ecuador, and Peru). Mexico was also ahead of the United States in enacting such legislation. Further, the approach taken in the Act was to exclude highly migratory species from zonal jurisdiction and to assert that the only viable management plan for such species was through international agreement. As for shrimp, experience had shown that bilateral treaties for access into other countries' fishery zones can be negotiated. The shrimp fishing agreement between the United States and Brazil is one example. Since the Act indicates that the United States was willing to accept traditional fishing rights of foreign nations within its extended fisheries zone, it was hoped that we would be able to exact reciprocity from other nations for recognition of traditional United States fishing rights.

Opponents of the Act claimed that neither the Soviet Union nor Japan was likely to recognize the validity of an extended United States fisheries zone claim and that as a result we would be required to enforce the law against vessels of these nations, a situation that could lead to confrontation and possibly to economic retaliation and a weakening of U.S.–Japan and U.S.–U.S.S.R. relations. Proponents pointed to evidence that both the Japanese and the Soviets were negotiating with United States fisheries interests for joint venture arrangements should the United States decide to totally exclude foreign fishing by flag vessels of those two nations. This presumably evidenced an intent not to engage in confrontation but rather to negotiate a way around a potentially dangerous situation. Further, proponents argued that total exclusion was extremely unlikely, and that what the United States really sought through the Act was a management program for fisheries within the 200-mile zone that would impose certain regulations on fishing effort there (and perhaps reduction of effort) but that would not exclude foreign fishing entirely. Finally, even if the Third LOS Conference were to produce an agreement, the financial and political costs of enforcement would have to be faced anyway—a unilaterally established zone only accelerated the time at which such expenditures would have to be made.

As noted, the proponents carried the day, and on April 13, 1976, the Fishery Conservation and Management Act became law.

Major Provision of the Act

The Fishery Conservation and Management Act of 1976 consists of four titles: Title I—"Fishery Management Authority of the United States;" Title II—"Foreign Fishing and International Fishery Agreements;" Title III—"National Fishery Management Program;" and Title IV—"Miscellaneous Provisions." Title I and the enforcement provisions (§§307, 308, 309, 310, and 311) entered into legal effect on March 1, 1977. The remainder of the major provisions became effective on the date of enactment (excerpts from the Act are set forth in Annex D to this book).

Fishery Management Authority of the United States. Section 101 establishes a fishery conservation zone extending from the seaward boundary of each coastal state to a line 200 nautical miles from the baseline from which the territorial sea is measured. The United States exercises "exclusive fishery management authority" with respect to all fish within the zone, all anadromous species throughout their migratory range (except within a foreign nation's territorial sea or recognized fishery conservation zone), and all continental shelf fishery resources beyond the zone. Highly migratory species (e.g., tuna) are specifically exempted from coverage of the management authority within the zone. The effective date of the enforcement provisions is March 1, 1977, that date having been selected as a compromise between the House version (July 1, 1976) and the Senate version (July 1, 1977). The President's agreement to sign the bill was predicated in large part on the deferred effective date.

Foreign Fishing and International Fishery Agreements. Foreign fishing in the zone is prohibited unless it is authorized by an existing fishery treaty or agreement or by a "governing international fishery agreement" (a treaty or an executive agreement) negotiated pursuant to the Act. Each fishing vessel of a nation authorized to fish within the zone must have a valid permit and must fish in accordance with the conditions and restrictions of that permit.

Foreign fishing may continue pursuant to and in accordance with fishery treaties or agreements in effect on March 1, 1977, that have not been renegotiated or that have not otherwise ceased to be in effect with respect to the United States. The Secretary of State has a duty to renegotiate such treaties pertaining to fishing within the conservation zone (or anadromous or continental shelf species beyond such zones) that are in any manner inconsistent with the purposes, policy, or provisions of the Act. Agreements may not be renewed except as set forth in the Act, as described below.

"Governing international fishery agreements" (GIFA) are to be negotiated with any nations desiring access to the exclusive fishery zone (or to anadromous or sedentary species subject to United States jurisdiction) after the effective date of the Act or after the expiration of existing agreements. Permits for individual vessels will only be issued to vessels of nations that are parties to a GIFA with the United States. Such agreements must acknowledge the exclusive fishery management authority of the United States and must include a binding commitment on the part of the foreign nation and its fishing vessels to comply with a wide range of conditions including regulations promulgated by the Secretary of Commerce pursuant to the Act; provisions for boarding, searching, and inspecting the vessels engaged in fishing activities within the zone; compliance with allocations of allowable levels of foreign fishing; and assurances that the nation will take steps under its own law to assure that permit holders comply with applicable conditions and restrictions. Foreign fishing is not, however, to be authorized for vessels of any nation unless that nation satisfies the United States that it extends substantially the same fishing privileges to vessels of the United States as the United States extends to foreign fishing vessels.

GIFA's in the form of executive agreements (i.e., those not submitted to the Senate as treaties for its advice and consent pursuant to the Constitution) are made subject to review and disapproval by the Congress. Each such agreement must be forwarded to the Congress and may not become effective for sixty days after it is so transmitted. Congress may disapprove the agreement by passage of a joint resolution. Presumably Congress could make a GIFA effective prior to the expiration of the sixty-day period by taking affirmative action to that effect in the form of a joint resolution.

The total allowable level of foreign fishing is that portion of the optimum yield of the fishery that will not be harvested by vessels of the United States, as determined in accordance with the management plan in effect. Allocation of the allowable level of foreign fishing is to be made by the Secretary of State, in cooperation with the Secretary of Commerce, taking into consideration: (1) traditional fishing activities; (2) cooperation with the United States in fishery research, enforcement, conservation, and management of fishery resources; and (3) such other matters as the Secretary of State and Secretary of Commerce deem appropriate.

The act contains a "sense of the Congress" provisions that the United States govenment should not recognize the claim of foreign fishery conservation zones by nations that fail to take into account traditional fishing activities of fishing vessels of the United States, fail to recognize and accept that highly migratory species are to be managed by applicable international fishery agreements (whether or not such nation is a party to any such agreements), or impose on fishing vessels of the United States any conditions or restrictions that are unrelated to fishery conservation and management. This provision was designed to protect the tuna fishing industry by permitting the Fishermen's Protective Act to remain applicable to tunaboat seizures within 200 miles of a nation's coast. The United States could no longer take the position that 200-mile fishing zones were *per se* illegal, since it now claims one of its own. However, by excluding highly migratory species from coverage in the Act, the United States remains in a position to argue that such species are legally managed only by international agreements and may not be subject to the exclusive jurisdiction of a coastal state beyond a 12-mile limit.

Permits for foreign fishing are obtained by application of a foreign nation (with which the United States has entered into a GIFA) to the Secretary of State on an annual basis for each fishing vessel that wishes to engage in fishing within the zone (or for anadromous or continental shelf species beyond the zone). Applications must be stock specific and provide detailed information about the fishing effort to be undertaken as well as the area, season, or period during which the fishing will occur. The application must be published in the Federal Register, with copies provided to the Secretary of Commerce, the appropriate regional management councils, the Secretary of Transportation (for the Coast Guard), the House Committee on Merchant Marine and Fisheries, and the Senate Committees on Commerce and Foreign Relations. Approval of permit application is obtained through a process of consultation among all parties to whom copies are transmitted, and the Secretary of Commerce is authorized to establish the conditions and restrictions to be included in the permit. Disapprovals are to be communicated to foreign nations by the Secretary of State. Reasonable fees are to be paid to the Secretary of Commerce by the owner or operator of vessels to whom a permit is issued pursuant to the Act. Violations of the Act may subject the permit owner to permit revocation or suspension, or imposition of additional conditions and restrictions.

Finally, if a foreign nation (1) does not allow United States vessels access to its fishery conservation zone on the same terms and conditions as foreign vessels are admitted to the United States fishery conservation zone, (2) does not permit United States vessels to engage in fishing for highly migratory species in accordance with applicable international fishery agreements (whether or not such nation is a party to that agreement), (3) does not comply with obligations under existing fishery agreement, or (4) seizes a United States fishing vessel in violation of a treaty or international law, the Secretary of the Treasury is required to prohibit the importation of fish and fish products from the fishery involved and may prohibit the importation of other fish and fish products from the country involved.

National Fishery Management Program. This title of the Act provides the mechanism for the implementation of a management program for fishery resources subject to the jurisdiction of the United States under the Act. Management plans prepared pursuant to the Act, as well as regulations promulgated pursuant thereto, are to be consistent with seven enumerated national standards for fishery conservation and management. The seven standards relate to prevention of overfishing, achieving optimal yield from each fishery, utilization of the best scientific information available, management of fish throughout their migratory range, treatment of interrelated stocks as unit, nondiscrimination among residents of different states, promotion of efficiency in the utilization of fishery resources, recognition of the variations among and contingencies in fishery resources and catches, and minimization of costs and avoidance of unnecessary duplication.

The Act establishes eight regional fishery management councils (New England, Mid-Atlantic, South Atlantic, Caribbean, Gulf, Pacific, North Pacific, and Western Pacific) the membership of which is to reflect the expertise and interests of the several constituent states in ocean areas over which the Council is granted authority. Each Council has a designated number of voting members, which is to include principal state officials with marine fishery management responsibility in the constituent states, the regional director of the National Marine Fisheries Service of the geographic area concerned, and members appointed by the Secretary of Commerce from a list of qualified individuals submitted by the Governor of each applicable constituent state. The Council also will include nonvoting members from various federal agencies including the United States Fish and Wildlife Service, the Coast Guard, and the Department of State.

The Regional Councils (as well as the Secretary of Commerce) are authorized to prepare fishery management plans containing conservation and management measures applicable to foreign and domestic fishing activities. Any fishery management plan submitted by a Regional Council to the Secretary of Commerce is to be reviewed within sixty days, and the Secretary must notify the Council in writing of the approval, disapproval, or partial disapproval of the plan. In cases of disapproval or partial disapproval the Secretary must include a statement and explanation of the objections, and reasons therefor, together with suggestions for improvements and a request to the Council to modify the plan or amendment. In reviewing a management plan submitted by a Council, the Secretary is to determine whether the plan is consistent with the specified national standards, other provisions of the Act, and any other applicable laws. The Secretary of Commerce must consult with the Secretary of State with respect to foreign fishing and the Secretary of Transportation (for the Coast Guard) with respect to enforcement.

The Secretary of Commerce may prepare fishery management plans if the appropriate Council fails to develop and submit such a plan within a reasonable time or if the Secretary disapproves or partially disapproves of any such plan and the Council involved fails to change the plan in accordance with the Act. In cases where the Secretary of Commerce prepares the plan he is required to transmit it to the appropriate Council for consideration and comment, and the Council is given forty-five days to recommend changes in the plan or amendment thereof. However, the Secretary of Commerce is not authorized to include a limited entry system in the plan unless that system is first approved by a majority of the members present and voting of the appropriate Council.

The Act also contains provisions concerning the preparation of regulations to implement fishery management plans, including notice in the Federal Register, public hearings, judicial review, and annual reports. Further, nothing in the Act is to be construed as extending or diminishing the jurisdiction or authority of any state within its boundaries, provided that if a state has taken action or omitted to take action the results of which would substantially and adversely affect the carrying out of a fishery management plan in the fishery conservation zone (or beyond it) the Secretary of Commerce is authorized to notify the state and the appropriate Regional Council of that finding and of the intention to regulate the applicable fishery within the boundaries of that state (excluding its internal waters). This power to preempt state management authority within state boundaries is limited to fisheries that are predominantly located in the fishery conservation zone or beyond.

The provisions of the Act are to be enforced by the Secretary of Commerce and the Secretary of the department in which the Coast Guard is operating, although both Secretaries are authorized to utilize the personnel, services, equipment, and facilities of any other federal agency including all elements of the Department of Defense or any state agency. Authorized enforcement officers are permitted to enforce the provisions of the Act by arrest, boarding, search, inspection, and seizure of vessels, fish, or other evidence, all with or without a warrant or other process.

Details concerning the method of operation of the Regional Councils were still sketchy as of this writing. However, interim regulations were published in the September 15, 1976, issue of the Federal Register.[23] These regulations cover such matters as uniform standards for organization, administrative practices and procedures, and operations practices and procedures. Also set forth are guidelines for development of fishery management plans. A fishery management plan is defined in the regulations as:

A document that contains a systematic description of a given fishery, including present conditions and past history, and that sets forth the objectives and strategies for the management of the fishery, including recommended allocations to users, and specifies the practical conservation and management measures needed to achieve those objectives. It is a discrete and essential element of the national fishery management program, and when implemented, is controlling as to the utilization of a given fishery.[24]

Miscellaneous Provision. If the United States should ratify a comprehensive law of the sea treaty including provisions with respect to fishery conservation and management, the Secretary of Commerce, after consultation with the Secretary of State, is authorized to promulgate amendments to regulations promulgated under the Act if that is necessary and appropriate to conform the regulations to provisions of the treaty.

Amendments to the Fishermen's Protective Act would conform it to the provisions of the Act and maintain it in force in situations where United States vessels are not accorded the same treatment by foreign countries as foreign vessels would be accorded under the Act within the United States fishery conservation zone.

Finally, both the 12-mile Exclusive Fisheries Zone Act of 1966 and the Bartlett Act are repealed.

Responses to the Act

As expected, the two major distant-water fishing nations, the Soviet Union and Japan, immediately transmitted notes of protest concerning the enactment of the 200-mile fisheries zone bill. The Japanese note is worth quoting in full:

The Embassy of Japan presents its compliments to the Department of State and, under instructions of its home Government, has the honor to express the regrets of the Government of Japan over the recent enactment of the Fishery Conservation and Management Act of 1976, in consonance with the previously stated position of the Government of Japan that all nations should refrain from taking measures to establish unilaterally a two hundred nautical mile exclusive fishery zone prior to the conclusion of the Law of the Sea Conference.

The Embassy further has the honor to state the position of the Government of Japan that the unilateral establishment of exclusive fishery management authority based on the above-mentioned Act cannot be deemed valid under international law and that the traditional interests of the Japanese fishing industry on the high seas should not be injured on account of the unilateral action of the Government of the United States.

The Soviet note was in similar vein, but was delivered "unofficially" thus making a less strong objection than the Japanese note.

Such protests are designed, of course, to affect both national policy and the development of international law. At the national policy level, the protest sought to urge the United State to repeal the act (an unlikelihood), to secure nonenforcement against Japanese fishermen (also unlikely), or to make the degree of Japan's interests in high seas fisheries off the United States coast known in order to lay the groundwork for future negotiations. The latter point is well understood by the United States Government and may affect the terms of any GIFA negotiated with Japan.

Internationally, Japan's protest is designed to attenuate the development of a rule of customary international law validating 200-mile exclusive fishing zones. Concurrent state practice over a long period of time, with the acquiescence of the majority of the nations of the world, can ripen into binding law. A paper protest has some moderating influence on this development process, although the regular insertion of fishing vessels (such as by the United States in the U.S.-CEP dispute) has an even greater impact on the possibilities for customary law development.

In view of development at the Third LOS Conference and in a growing number of coastal states, it appears that the Japanese action will be ineffective. More likely, the practice of nations dealing with the United States zone will establish the details of customary law at sometime in the future. It is important, then, to examine the first GIFA negotiated under the Fishery Conservation and Management Act of 1976, the United States-Poland treaty.

The First "Governing International Fisheries Agreement" Negotiations

Shortly after the Fishery Conservation and Management Act of 1976 (FCMA) became law, the United States began negotiations with a number of countries in order to adopt governing international fishery agreements (GIFA) as required by the new law. These talks were conducted on behalf of the United States by the Office of the Assistant Secretary of State for Oceans and Environmental and Scientific Affairs. Negotiations were undertaken with Bulgaria, Romania, Poland, the Soviet Union, South Korea, Japan, Canada, Mexico, and the Republic of China, among others. The first agreed text was between the United States and Poland.[25] On September 16, 1976, in accordance with the FCMA, the President transmitted to the Congress the text of the Polish agreement and in his message accompanying the agreement stated that:

This Agreement is significant because it is the first to be negotiated in accordance with the legislation. I recommend the Congress give favorable consideration to this Agreement at an early date. I recommend that, in the event 60 calendar days of continuous session as required by the legislation are not available before March 1, 1977, the Congress consider issuance of a joint resolution in order to bring this Agreement into force by that date.[26]

Since Congress adjourned on October 2, 1976, the period from September 16 to October 2 did not meet the requirement of "60 calendar days of continuous session." Since Congress reconvened on January 4, 1977, the sixty continuous calendar days expire on March 5, four days after the enforcement provisions of the FCMA become effective. In making the recommendation that Congress act affirmatively by a joint resolution, the President was seeking to ensure that the

Polish Agreement would be in force and permits issued thereunder on the date that the Act's enforcement provisions became effective. Otherwise, there would be a period during which it would be illegal under the FCMA for Polish vessels to fish within the 200-mile zone. At the time of this writing (October 1976) it was uncertain whether Congress would be disposed to accede the President's request. Some members of Congress indicated that they wanted to take a long and careful look at the Polish GIFA, since it was the first such agreement and would undoubtedly set the pattern for future agreements. That review process could well take the entire sixty days of continuous session beginning in January 1977.

Summary of Provisions

At the outset, and as required by the FCMA, Poland acknowledges in the preambulary recitations the fishery management authority of the United States in the 200-mile zone. It is this recognition requirement that will probably be a major stumbling block in negotiations with Japan since that nation has extensive distant-water fishing activities throughout the world, and its acknowledgement of United States 200-mile fishery jurisdiction could have adverse impacts beyond United States coastal fishery operations. Countries with more modest foreign fishing commitments are less likely to be perturbed by this requirement of the FCMA.

The stated purpose of the Agreement is to "ensure effective conservation, optimum utilization, rational management" of fisheries off the coast of the United States and to establish the principles and procedures by which Polish nationals will be permitted to engage in fishing activities within the exclusive fishery zone.[27]

The United States indicates its willingness to allow access for Polish fishing vessels to operate within the zone pursuant to the permits to be issued and subject to a determination by the United States of the amount of the allowable catch applicable to Poland. The process by which the Polish quota is to be established consists of four steps, all within United States discretion: (1) a determination of the total allowable catch for each fishery, (2) a determination of the harvesting capacity of United States fishing vessels for each fishery, (3) a determination of that portion of total allowable catch that will not be harvested by United States vessels for each fishery, and (4) the allocation of that portion not to be harvested by U.S. fishing vessels that can be made available to qualifying Polish vessels. The United States is also authorized to determine measures necessary to achieve an optimum yield from each fishery while avoiding overfishing. Such measures include traditional conservation techniques such as closed areas, closed seasons, size and catch limitations, restrictions on effort, and gear restrictions.[28]

The United States commits itself to a management objective of "optimum utilization" and establishes criteria by which surplus fishery stocks may be made available to vessels of other countries. Those criteria include the following factors relative to the conduct of foreign nations: (1) traditional fishing activities, if any, (2) contributions to fishery research and the identification of fish stocks, (3) previous cooperation in enforcement, (4) previous cooperation with respect to conservation and management of fishery resources of mutual concern, and (5) the need to minimize economic dislocation in cases where vessels have habitually fished for living resources over which the United States now exercises fishery management authority.[29] Obviously, there is a good deal of room for subjective judgment in these criteria, yet all of them appear to be rationally related to the objectives of the FCMA, viz., the proper conservation, management, and utilization of coastal fishery resources.

Subsequent articles specify the obligations undertaken by Poland, which are essentially to refrain from fishing except pursuant to the Agreement and permits issued thereunder, to ensure that authorized vessels comply with the provisions of their permits when issued, and to comply with conservation regulations in force.[30] Compliance with marine mammal protection laws is also required.[31] Finally, Poland agrees to certain technical requirements concerning display of permits, maintenance of position-fixing equipment on vessels, and permissibility of boarding and inspection by United States enforcement agents.[32]

The Agreement provides for Poland's right to submit an application for fishing permits for each Polish fishing vessel wishing to engage in fishing the zone and provides that the applications are to be prepared and processed in accordance with detailed provisions set forth in Annex I to the agreement.[33]

Annex I provides that applications for permits must specify (1) the name and number of each fishing vessel, (2) a description of the vessel and the type of fishing gear carried, (3) a specification of each fishery in which the vessel wishes to fish, (4) the amount of fish contemplated to be caught during the permit term, (5) the area and season in which the fishing will be conducted, and (6) "such other relevant information as may be requested."[34] The United States then reviews the application and makes a determination as to what conditions, restrictions, and fees will be imposed on issuance of permits. After the United States informs Poland of those determinations, Poland has the option to accept or reject the conditions. Should it reject the conditions, it is required to state its objections. In the case of an objection by Poland to the conditions and restrictions, the governments are to negotiate after which Poland may submit a revised application.

Upon the acceptance of the permit conditions and restrictions, and the payment of any fees due, the United States is obligated to approve the application and issue a permit. The permits are to be issued for a specific vessel and are not transferable.

Another annex to the agreement continues the establishment of the

American-Polish fisheries board, which considers claims advanced by nationals of either state against nationals of the other regarding financial loss resulting from damage to or a loss of that nationals' fishing vessel or fishing gear.[35] Still another annex concerns data collection and reporting requirements for Polish vessels, the intent of which is to provide to the United States as much information as possible about the fisheries off its coast.[36] Finally, the agreement is terminated by a set of "agreed minutes" concerned primarily with the transition between the existing regime of high seas fishing and the regulatory system imposed pursuant to the FCMA.[37]

As noted above, this type of agreement is apt to become standard fare for nations wishing to fish within 200 miles of the coast of the United States. In that regard it is interesting to note that in spite of the dire predictions made by the State Department when it opposed enactment of the FCMA, the vast majority of nations that have fishing interests off the United States coasts have indicated their willingness to negotiate and sign agreements such as that just described. The outcome of the FCMA is therefore much more likely to be a peaceful transition to a property rights system for the management of living marine resources than a new semipermanent era of conflict in the ocean.

Notes

1. A portion of this section was originally published by the author in vol. 6, no. 1, of the *Georgia Journal of International and Comparative Law* (Winter 1976). It is reproduced here, in revised form, with permission of the Georgia Journal of International and Comparative Law, Inc.

2. Policy of the United States with Respect to Coastal Fisheries in Certain Areas of the High Seas, Pres. Proc. No. 2668, 3 C.F.R. 68 (1954–1948 Comp.), reprinted in 13 *Department of State Bulletin* 486 (1945).

3. *Fishermen's Protective Act*, 22 U.S.C. §§1971–1979 (originally enacted August 27, 1954; 68 Stat. 883).

4. *Exclusive Fisheries Zone Act*, 16 U.S.C. §§1091–1094 (originally enacted October 14, 1966; P.L. 89–658).

5. *Bartlett Act*, 16 U.S.C. §1081 *et seq.* (originally enacted May 20, 1964; 78 Stat. 194).

6. *Agreement with Canada on Reciprocal Fishing Privileges in Certain Areas off Their Coasts*, June 15, 1973, [1973] 2 U.S.T. 1729, T.I.A.S. No. 7676 (effective June 16, 1973).

7. *Agreement with Mexico on Traditional Fishing in the Exclusive Fishery Zones Contiguous to the Territorial Seas of Both Countries*, Oct. 17, 1967, [1967] 3 U.S.T. 2724, T.I.A.S. No. 6359 (effective Jan. 1, 1968). This agreement is no longer in force.

8. See, e.g., *Agreement with the Soviet Union on Certain Fishery Problems on the High Seas in the Western Areas of the Middle Atlantic Ocean*, Dec. 11, 1970, [1970] 3 U.S.T. 2664, T.I.A.S. No. 7009 (effective Jan. 1, 1971). See generally Eugene R. Fidell, "Ten Years Under the Bartlett Act: A Status Report on the Prohibition of Foreign Fishing," *Boston University Law Review* 54 (1974): 703-756, 708-713; and David W. Windley, "International Practice Regarding Traditional Fishing Privileges of Foreign Fishermen in Zones of Extended Maritime Jurisdiction," *American Journal of International Law* 63 (1969): 490-503.

9. *Offshore Shrimp Fisheries Act of 1973*, P.L. 93-242; 87 Stat. 1061. The species so listed, as well as other not included in the Act, had previously been designated by administrative action. See 50. C.F.R., Pt. 295 (1973).

10. Guidelines for Enforcement of United States Rights to Continental Shelf Fishery Resources, Department of State Press Release No. 363 (Sept. 12, 1974). These guidelines were promulgated in the form of federal regulations on June 24, 1976. See 41 *Fed. Reg.* 26019 (June 24, 1976).

11. *Hearings before the Subcommittee on Fisheries and Wildlife Conservation and the Environment of the House Committee on Merchant Marine and Fisheries on Extending the Jurisdiction of the United States Beyond the Present Twelve-Mile Fishery Zone* (93d Cong., 2d Sess., May 10-October 18, 1974), Serial No. 93-97.

12. *Hearings before the Subcommittee on Oceans and Atmosphere of the Senate Committee on Commerce on S. 1988, et al.* (93d Cong., 2d Sess., February 11-April 1, 1974), Part 2, Serial No. 93-54; *Hearing before the Senate Committee on Foreign Relations on S. 1988* (93d Cong., 2d Sess., September 5, 1974); *Hearing before the Senate Committee on Armed Services on S. 1988* (93d Cong., 2d Sess., October 8, 9, and 11, 1974).

13. *Report of the Senate Committee on Commerce on S. 1988*, S. Rept. no. 93-1079 (August 8, 1974); *Report of the Senate Committee on Foreign Relations on the Emergency Marine Fisheries Protection Act*, S. Rept. No. 93-1166 (September 23, 1974); *Report of the Committee on Armed Services on the Emergency Marine Fisheries Protection Act of 1974*, S. Rept. 93-1300 (November 27, 1974).

14. *Hearings before the Subcommittee on Fisheries and Wildlife Conservation and the Environment of the House Committee on Merchant Marine and Fisheries on H.R. 200, et al.* (94th Cong., 1st Sess., March 10, 11, 12, 13, 14, 18, 20, 27, 1975), Serial No. 94-4.

15. "Potential Impact of the Proposed 200-Mile Fishing Zone on U.S. Foreign Relations," *Special Oversight Report of the House Committee on International Relations* (94th Cong., 1st Sess., October 8, 1975), H. Rept. 94-542.

16. *Hearing before the Senate Committee on Commerce on S. 961* (94th Cong., 1st Sess., June 6 and September 19, 1975), parts 1 and 2, Serial No. 94-27.

17. *Hearing before the Subcommittee on Oceans and International Environment of the Senate Committee on Foreign Relations on S. 961* (94th Cong., 1st Sess., October 31, 1975).

18. *Hearing before the Senate Committee on Armed Services on S. 961* (94th Cong., 1st sess., November 19, 1975).

19. Commerce—Senate Report No. 94–416 (94th Cong., 1st Sess., October 7, 1975); Foreign Relations—Senate Report No. 94–459 (94th Cong., 1st Sess., November 18, 1975); Armed Services—Senate Report No. 94–515 (94th Cong., 1st Sess., December 8, 1975).

20. "Fishery Conservation and Management Act of 1976," *Report of the Committee of Conference on H.R. 200* (94th Cong., 2d Sess., March 24, 1976).

21. 12 Wkly. Comp. Pres. Docs. (no. 15; April 19, 1976).

22. *A Legislative History of the Fishery Conservation and Management Act of 1976* together with a section-by-section index (94th Cong. 2d Sess., October, 1976) (Superintendent of Documents, U.S. Government Printing Office, Washington, D.C. 20402).

23. Fishery Conservation and Management, National Oceanic and Atmospheric Administration, Department of Commerce: Regional Fishery Management Councils—Interim Regulations, 41 *Fed. Reg.* 39436 (September 15, 1976). See also "Draft Foreign Fishing Regulations," 41 *Fed. Reg.* 55904 (December 23, 1976).

24. Ibid., §601.2(a), p. 39436.

25. *Agreement Between the Government of the United States of America and the Government of the Polish People's Republic Concerning Fisheries off the Coasts of the United States,* House Doc. 94–613 (signed August 2, 1976; transmitted to the Congress by the President on September 16, 1976).

26. 122 *Cong. Rcd.* S15943 (daily ed. September 16, 1976).

27. *Agreement Between the United States and Poland,* op. cit., art. 1.

28. Ibid., art. 3.

29. Ibid, art. 4.

30. Ibid., art. 5.

31. Ibid., art. 7.

32. Ibid., arts. 8, 9.

33. Ibid., art. 6.

34. Ibid., Annex 1, para. 1–2.

35. Ibid., Annex 2.

36. Ibid., Annex 3.

37. Ibid., Agreed Minutes.

7 Conclusion

By now the reader should have a good perspective on the development of international fisheries management, sufficient in any case to understand the nature of and reasons for the current conflicts over fisheries jurisdiction. There can be little doubt that, insofar as fisheries are concerned, the law of the sea is well into its fourth and final phase—the creation of property rights. Whether through international agreement at the Third UN Conference on the Law of the Sea, or by the unilateral enactment of domestic legislation by coastal states, exclusive jurisdiction over most fish stocks will be accorded to coastal states.

That being the case, a jurisdictional base for management will have been established. For the first time, states will have the opportunity to avoid biologic and economic waste—to avoid the tragedy of the commons. Whether they will do so cannot be foretold at present, although the concepts for management set forth in the United States' "Fishery Conservation and Management Act of 1976" offer hope that a rational fishery management system can be developed for that nation's fisheries. Other countries should carefully follow management programs promulgated under the FCMA with a view toward emulating the successful aspects and eliminating the unsuccessful efforts. Hopefully, in this manner, the FCMA can become a basis for sound management of marine fisheries.

Annex A:
Table of Fishing Limits of
Independent Countries

(From "Limits in the Seas: National Claims to Maritime Jurisdictions, "no. 36, 3d rev., December 23, 1975, Office of the Geographer, Bureau of Intelligence and Research, Department of State)

Three-Mile Fishing Limit (14)

Bahrain	Germany, Fed. Rep.	Jordan
Barbados	German Dem. Rep.	Qatar
China, (ROC)	Grenada	Singapore
Cuba	Guyana	United Arab Emirates
Fiji	Japan	(except Sarjah)

Four-Mile Fishing Limit (1)

Finland

Six-Mile Fishing Limit (3)

Greece	Israel	Lebanon

Twelve-Mile Fishing Limit (75)

Albania	Equatorial Guinea	Libya
Algeria	Ethiopia	Malaysia
Angola	France	Mauritius
Australia	Guatemala	Monaco
Bahamas, The	Guinea	Mozambique
Belgium	Honduras	Nauru
Benin (Dahomey)	India	Netherlands
Burma	Indonesia	New Zealand
Cambodia	Iraq	Norway
Canada	Ireland	Papua New Guinea
Cape Verde	Italy	Poland
China, (PRC)	Ivory Coast	Portugal
Colombia	Jamaica	Romania
Comoro Islands	Kenya	Sao Tome and
Cyprus	Korea, North	Principe
Denmark	Korea, Rep. of	Saudi Arabia
Domican Rep.	Kuwait	South Africa
Egypt	Liberia	Soviet Union

Twelve-Mile Fishing Limit (75) *(Continued)*

Spain
Sri Lanka
Sudan
Surinam
Sweden
Syria
Thailand

Togo
Trinidad and Tobago
Tunisia
Turkey
  (Ukranian SSR)
United
  Kingdom

Venezuela
Vietnam (N)
Western Samoa
Yemen (Aden)
Yemen (Sana)
Yugoslavia
Zaire

Fifteen-Mile Fishing Limit (1)

Haiti

Eighteen-Mile Fishing Limit (1)

Cameroon

Twenty-Mile Fishing Limit (1)

Malta

Thirty-Mile Fishing Limit (4)

Congo
Ghana

Mauritania
Nigeria

Fifty-Mile Fishing Limit (6)

Gambia, The
Iran

Madagascar
Oman

Pakistan
Tanzania

Fifty-Three-Mile Fishing Limit (1)

Vietnam, Rep. of

Seventy-Mile Fishing Limit (1)

Morocco

One-Hundred-Thirty-Mile Fishing Limit (1)

Guinea

One-Hundred-Thirty-Two-Mile Fishing Limit (1)

Senegal

One-Hundred-Fifty-Mile Fishing Limit (2)

Gabon   Guinea-Bissau

Two-Hundred-Mile Fishing Limit (13)

Argentina	El Salvador	Peru
Bangladesh	Iceland	Sierra Leone
Brazil	Mexico	Somalia
Chile	Nicaragua	United States (as of March 1, 1977)
Ecuador	Panama	Uruguay

Modified Archipelago (3)

Maldives   Philippines   Tonga

"Specialized Competence" over Living Resources to 200 Miles (1)

Costa Rica

Land-Locked (30)

Annex B:
Agenda of the Third UN
Conference on the Law of
the Sea

United Nations Seabed Committee: List of Subjects and
Issues to Be Discussed at Law of the Sea Conference
(August 16, 1972)

1. International Regime for the Sea-Bed and the Ocean Floor Beyond
   National Jurisdiction
   1.1 Nature and Characteristics
   1.2 International Machinery: Structure, Functions, Powers
   1.3 Economic Implications
   1.4 Equitable Sharing of Benefits Bearing in Mind the Special Interests
       and Needs of the Developing Countries, Whether Coastal or Land-Locked
   1.5 Definition and Limits of the Area
   1.6 Use Exclusively for Peaceful Purposes
2. Territorial Sea
   2.1 Nature and Characteristics, Including the Question of the Unity or
       Plurality of Regimes in the Territorial Sea
   2.2 Historic Waters
   2.3 Limits
       2.3.1 Question of the Delimitation of the Territorial Sea: Various
             Aspects Involved
       2.3.2 Breadth of the Territorial Sea, Global or Regional Criteria, Open
             Seas, and Oceans, Semi-Enclosed Seas and Enclosed Seas
   2.4 Innocent Passage in the Territorial Sea
   2.5 Freedom of Navigation and Overflight Resulting from the Question
       of Plurality of Regimes in the Territorial Sea
3. Contiguous Zone
   3.1 Nature and Characteristics
   3.2 Limits
   3.3 Rights of Coastal States with Regard to National Security, Customs and
       Fiscal Control, Sanitation and Immigration Regulations
4. Straits Used for International Navigation
   4.1 Innocent Passage
   4.2 Other Related Matters Including the Question of the Right of Transit
5. Continental Shelf
   5.1 Nature and Scope of the Sovereign Rights of Coastal States Over the
       Continental Shelf, Duties of States
   5.2 Outer Limit of the Continental Shelf: Applicable Criteria
   5.3 Question of the Delimitation between States: Various Aspects Involved
   5.4 Natural Resources of the Continental Shelf
   5.5 Regime for Waters Superjacent to the Continental Shelf
   5.6 Scientific Research

14.1.3 Transfer of Technology to Developing Countries
15. Regional Arrangements
16. Archipelagoes
17. Enclosed and Semi-Enclosed Seas
18. Artificial Islands and Installations
19. Regime of Islands:
    (A)   Islands under Colonial Dependence or Foreign Domination or Control
    (B)   Other Related Matters
20. Responsibility and Liability for Damage Resulting from the Use of the Marine Environment
21. Settlement of Disputes
22. Peaceful Uses of the Ocean Space: Zones of Peace and Security
23. Archaeological and Historical Treasures on the Sea-Bed and Ocean Floor beyond the Limits of National Jurisdiction
24. Transmission from the High Seas
25. Enhancing the Universal Participation of States in Multilateral Conventions Relating to the Law of the Sea

Article 44

*Rights, Jurisdiction and Duties of the Coastal State in
Exclusive Economic Zone*

1. In an area beyond and adjacent to its territorial sea, described as the exclusive economic zone, the coastal State has:

(a) Sovereign rights for the purpose of exploring and exploiting, conserving and managing the natural resources, whether living or non-living, of the bed and subsoil and the superjacent waters;

(b) Exclusive rights and jurisdiction with regard to the establishment and use of artificial islands, installations and structures;

(c) Exclusive jurisdiction with regard to:

(i) Other activities for the economic exploitation and exploration of the zone, such as the production of energy from the water, currents and winds; and

(ii) Scientific research;

(d) Jurisdiction with regard to the preservation of the marine environment, including pollution control and abatement;

(e) Other rights and duties provided for in the present Convention.

2. In exercising its rights and performing its duties under the present Convention in the exclusive economic zone, the coastal State shall have due regard to the rights and duties of other States.

3. The rights set out in this article with respect to the bed and subsoil shall be exercised in accordance with Chapter IV. . . .

Article 50

Conservation of the Living Resources

1. The coastal State shall determine the allowable catch of the living resources in its exclusive economic zone.

2. The coastal State, taking into account the best scientific evidence available to it, shall ensure through proper conservation and management measures that the maintenance of the living resources in the exclusive economic zone is not endangered by over-exploitation. As appropriate the coastal State and relevant subregional, regional and global organizations shall co-operate to this end.

3. Such measures shall also be designed to maintain or restore populations

of harvested species at levels which can produce the maximum sustainable yield, as qualified by relevant environmental and economic factors, including the economic needs of coastal fishing communities and the special requirements of developing countries, and taking into account fishing patterns, the interdependence of stocks and any generally recommended subregional, regional or global minimum standards.

4. In establishing such measures the coastal State shall take into consideration the effects on species associated with or dependent upon harvested species with a view to maintaining or restoring populations of such associated or dependent species above levels at which their reproduction may become seriously threatened.

5. Available scientific information, catch and fishing effort statistics, and other data relevant to the conservation of fish stocks shall be contributed and exchanged on a regular basis through subregional, regional and global organizations where appropriate and with participation by all States concerned, including States whose nationals are allowed to fish in the exclusive economic zone.

Article 51

Utilization of the Living Resources

1. The coastal State shall promote the objective of optimum utilization of the living resources in the exclusive economic zone without prejudice to article 50.

2. The coastal State shall determine its capacity to harvest the living resources of the exclusive economic zone. Where the coastal State does not have the capacity to harvest the entire allowable catch, it shall, through agreements or other arrangements and pursuant to the terms, conditions and regulations referred to in paragraph 4, give other States access to the surplus of the allowable catch.

3. In giving access to other States to its exclusive economic zone under this article, the coastal State shall take into account all relevant factors, including *inter alia*, the significance of the renewable resources of the area to the economy of the coastal State concerned and its other national interests, the provisions of articles 58 and 59, the requirements of developing countries in the subregion or region in harvesting part of the surplus and the need to minimize economic dislocation in States whose nationals have habitually fished in the zone or which have made substantial efforts in research and identification of stocks.

4. Nationals of other States fishing in the exclusive economic zone shall comply with the conservation measures and with the other terms and conditions established in the regulations of the coastal State. These regulations shall be consistent with the present Convention and may relate, *inter alia,* to the following:

(a) Licensing of fishermen, fishing vessels and equipment, including payment of fees and other forms of remuneration, which in the case of developing coastal States, may consist of adequate compensation in the field of financing, equipment and technology relating to the fishing industry;

(b) Determining the species which may be caught, and fixing quotas of catch, whether in relation to particular stocks or groups of stocks or catch per vessel over a period of time or to the catch by nationals of any State during a specified period;

(c) Regulating seasons and areas of fishing, the types, sizes and amount of gear, and the numbers, sizes and types of fishing vessels that may be used;

(d) Fixing the age and size of fish and other species that may be caught;

(e) Specifying information required of fishing vessels, including catch and effort statistics and vessel position reports;

(f) Requiring, under the authorization and control of the coastal State, the conduct of specified fisheries research programmes and regulating the conduct of such research, including the sampling of catches, disposition of samples and reporting of associated scientific data;

(g) The placing of observers or trainees on board such vessels by the coastal State;

(h) The landing of all or any part of the catch by such vessels in the ports of the coastal State;

(i) Terms and conditions relating to joint ventures or other co-operative arrangements;

(j) Requirements for training personnel and transfer of fisheries technology, including enhancement of the coastal State's capability of undertaking fisheries research;

(k) Enforcement procedures.

5. Coastal States shall give due notice of conservation and management regulations.

Article 52

Stocks Occurring within the Exclusive Economic Zones
of Two or More Coastal States or Both within the
Exclusive Economic Zone and in an Area
Beyond and Adjacent to It

1. Where the same stock or stocks of associated species occur within the exclusive economic zones of two or more coastal States, these States shall seek either directly or through appropriate subregional or regional organizations to agree upon the measures necessary to co-ordinate and ensure the conservation and development of such stocks without prejudice to the other provisions of this Chapter.

2. Where the same stock or stocks of associated species occur both within the exclusive economic zone and in an area beyond and adjacent to the zone, the coastal State and the States fishing for such stocks in the adjacent area shall seek either directly or through appropriate subregional or regional organizations to agree upon the measures necessary for the conservation of these stocks in the adjacent area.

Article 53

High Migratory Species

1. The coastal State and other States whose nationals fish in the region for the highly migratory species listed in the annex shall co-operate directly or through appropriate international organizations with a view to ensuring conservation and promoting the objective of optimum utilization of such species throughout the region, both within and beyond the exclusive economic zone. In regions where no appropriate international organization exists, the coastal State and other States whose nationals harvest these species in the region shall co-operate to establish such an organization and participate in its work.

2. The provisions of paragraph 1 apply in addition to the other provisions of this Chapter.

Article 54

Marine Mammals

Nothing in the present Convention restricts the right of a coastal State or international organization, as appropriate, to prohibit, regulate and limit the exploitation of marine mammals. States shall co-operate either directly or through appropriate international organizations with a view to the protection and management of marine mammals.

Article 55

Anadromous Stocks

1. States in whose rivers anadromous stocks originate shall have the primary interest in and responsibility for such stocks.

2. The State of origin of anadromous stocks shall ensure their conservation by the establishment of appropriate regulatory measures for fishing in all

waters landwards of the outer limits of its exclusive economic zone and for fishing provided for in sub-paragraph 3(b). The State of origin may, after consultation with other States fishing these stocks, establish total allowable catches for stocks originating in its rivers.

3. (a) Fisheries for anadromous stocks shall be conducted only in the waters landwards of the outer limits of exclusive economic zones, except in cases where this provision would result in economic dislocation for a State other than the State of origin.

(b) The State of origin shall co-operate in minimizing economic dislocation in such other States fishing these stocks, taking into account the normal catch and the mode of operations of such States, and all the areas in which such fishing has occurred.

(c) States referred to in sub-paragraph (b), participating by agreement with the State of origin in measures to renew anadromous stocks, particularly by expenditures for that purpose, shall be given special consideration by the State of origin in the harvesting of stocks originating in its rivers.

(d) Enforcement of regulations regarding anadromous stocks beyond the exclusive economic zone shall be by agreement between the State of origin and the other States concerned.

4. In cases where anadromous stocks migrate into or through the waters landwards of the outer limits of the exclusive economic zone of a State other than the State of origin, such State shall co-operate with the State of origin with regard to the conservation and management of such stocks.

5. The State of origin of anadromous stocks and other States fishing these stocks shall make arrangements for the implementation of the provisions of this article where appropriate, through regional organizations.

Article 56

Catadromous Species

1. A coastal State in whose waters catadromous species spend the greater part of their life cycle shall have responsibility for the management of these species and shall ensure the ingress and egress of migrating fish.

2. Harvesting of catadromous species shall be conducted only in waters in respect of which the State mentioned in paragraph 1 exercises sovereign rights over the living resources and, when conducted in the exclusive economic zone, shall be subject to the provisions of the present Convention concerning fishing in the zone.

3. In cases where catadromous fish migrate through the waters of another State or States, whether as juvenile or maturing fish, the management, including harvesting, of such fish shall be regulated by agreement between the State

mentioned in paragraph 1 and the State or States concerned. Such agreement shall ensure the rational management of the species and take into account the responsibilities of the State mentioned in paragraph 1 for the maintenance of these species.

Article 57

Sedentary Species

This Chapter does not apply to sedentary species as defined in paragraph 4 of article 65.

Article 58

Right of Land-Locked States

1. Land-locked States shall have the right to participate in the exploitation of the living resources of the exclusive economic zones of adjoining coastal States on an equitable basis, taking into account the relevant economic and geographical circumstances of all the States concerned. The terms and conditions of such participation shall be determined by the States concerned through bilateral, subregional or regional agreements. Developed land-locked States shall, however, be entitled to exercise their rights only within the exclusive economic zones of adjoining developed coastal States.

2. This article is subject to the provisions of articles 50 and 51.

3. Paragraph 1 is without prejudice to arrangements agreed upon in regions where the coastal States may grant to land-locked States of the same region equal or preferential rights for the exploitation of the living resources in the exclusive economic zones.

Article 59

Right of Certain Developing Coastal States in a Subregion or Region

1. Developing coastal States which are situated in a subregion or region whose geographical peculiarities make such states particularly dependent for the satisfaction of the nutritional needs of their populations upon the exploitation of the living resources in the exclusive economic zones of their neighbouring States and developing coastal States which can claim no exclusive economic

zones of their own shall have the right to participate, on an equitable basis, in the exploitation of living resources in the exclusive economic zones of other States in a subregion or region.

2. The terms and conditions of such participation shall be determined by the States concerned through bilateral, subregional or regional agreements, taking into account the relevant economic and geographic circumstances of all the States concerned, including the need to avoid effects detrimental to the fishing communities or to the fishing industries of the States in whose zones the right of participation is exercised.

3. This article is subject to the provisions of article 50 and 51.

Sec. 2. Findings, Purposes and Policy

(a) *FINDINGS*. The Congress finds and declares the following:

(1) The fish off the coasts of the United States, the highly migratory species of the high seas, the species which dwell on or in the Continental Shelf appertaining to the United States, and the anadromous species which spawn in United States rivers or estuaries, constitute valuable and renewable natural resourses. These fishery resources contribute to the food supply, economy, and health of the Nation and provide recreational opportunities.

(2) As a consequence of increased fishing pressure and because of the inadequacy of fishery conservation and management practices and controls (A) certain stocks of such fish have been overfished to the point where their survival is threatened, and (B) other such stocks have been so substantially reduced in number that they could become similarly threatened.

(3) Commercial and recreational fishing constitutes a major source of employment and contributes significantly to the economy of the Nation. Many coastal areas are dependent upon fishing and related activities, and their economies have been badly damaged by the overfishing of fishery resources at an ever-increasing rate over the past decade. The activities of massive foreign fishing fleets in waters adjacent to such coastal areas have contributed to such damage, interfered with domestic fishing efforts, and caused destruction of the fishing gear of United States fishermen.

(4) International fishery agreements have not been effective in preventing or terminating the overfishing of these valuable fishery resources. There is danger that irreversible effects from overfishing will take place before an effective international agreement on fishery management jurisdiction can be negotiated, signed, ratified, and implemented.

(5) Fishery resources are finite but renewable. If placed under sound management before overfishing has caused irreversible effects, the fisheries can be conserved and maintained so as to provide optimum yields on a continuing basis.

(6) A national program for the conservation and management of the fishery resources of the United States is necessary to prevent overfishing, to rebuild overfished stocks, to insure conservation, and to realize the full potential of the Nation's fishery resources.

(7) A national program for the development of fisheries which are underutilized or not utilized by United States fishermen, including bottom fish off Alaska, is necessary to assure that our citizens benefit from the employment, food supply, and revenue which could be generated thereby.

(b) *PURPOSES.* It is therefore declared to be the purposes of the Congress in this Act:

(1) to take immediate action to conserve and manage the fishery resources found off the coasts of the United States, and the anadromous species and Continental Shelf fishery resources of the United States, by establishing (A) a fishery conservation zone within which the United States will assume exclusive fishery management authority over all fish, except highly migratory species, and (B) exclusive fishery management authority beyond such zone over such anadromous species and Continental Shelf fishery resources;

(2) to support and encourage the implementation and enforcement of international fishery agreements for the conservation and management of highly migratory species, and to encourage the negotiation and implementation of additional such agreements as necessary;

(3) to promote domestic commercial and recreational fishing under sound conservation and management principles;

(4) to provide for the preparation and implementation, in accordance with national standards, of fishery management plans which will achieve and maintain, on a continuing basis, the optimum yield from each fishery;

(5) to establish Regional Fishery Management Councils to prepare, monitor, and revise such plans under circumstances (A) which will enable the States, the fishing industry, consumer and environmental organizations, and other interested persons to participate in, and advise on, the establishment and administration of such plans, and (B) which take into account the social and economic needs of the States; and

(6) to encourage the development of fisheries which are currently underutilized or not utilized by United States fishermen, including bottom fish off Alaska.

(c) *POLICY.* It is further declared to be the policy of the Congress in this Act:

(1) to maintain without change the existing territorial or other ocean jurisdiction of the United States for all purposes other than the conservation and management of fishery resources, as provided for in this Act;

(2) to authorize no impediment to, or interference with, recognized legitimate uses of the high seas, except as necessary for the conservation and management of fishery resources, as provided for in this Act;

(3) to assure that the national fishery conservation and management program utilizes, and is based upon, the best scientific information available; involves, and is responsive to the needs of, interested and affected States and citizens; promotes efficiency; draws upon Federal, State, and academic capabilities in carrying out research, administration, management, and enforcement; and is workable and effective;

(4) to permit foreign fishing consistent with the provisions of this Act; and

(5) to support and encourage continued active United States efforts to obtain an internationally acceptable treaty, at the Third United Nations

Conference on the Law of the Sea, which provides for effective conservation and management of fishery resources.

Sec. 3. Definitions

As used in this Act, unless the context otherwise requires:

(1) The term "anadromous species" means species of fish which spawn in fresh or estuarine waters of the United States and which migrate to ocean waters.

(2) The term "conservation and management" refers to all of the rules, regulations, conditions, methods, and other measures (A) which are required to rebuild, restore, or maintain, and which are useful in rebuilding, restoring, or maintaining, any fishery resource and the marine environment; and (b) which are designed to assure that:

(i) a supply of food and other products may be taken, and that recreational benefits may be obtained, on a continuing basis;

(ii) irreversible or long-term adverse effects on fishery resources and the marine environment are avoided; and

(iii) there will be a multiplicity of options available with respect to future uses of these resources.

(3) The term "Continental Shelf" means the seabed and subsoil of the submarine areas adjacent to the coast, but outside the area of the territorial sea, of the United States to a depth of 200 meters or, beyond that limit, to where the depth of the superjacent waters admits of the exploitation of the natural resources of such areas. . . .

(6) The term "fish" means finfish, mollusks, crustaceans, and all other forms of marine animal and plant life other than marine mammals, birds, and highly migratory species.

(7) The term "fishery" means:

(A) one or more stocks of fish which can be treated as a unit for purposes of conservation and management and which are identified on the basis of geographical, scientific, technical, recreational, and economic characteristics; and

(B) any fishing for such stocks.

(8) The term "fishery conservation zone" means the fishery conservation zone established by section 101.

(9) The term "fishery resource" means any fishery, any stock of fish, any species of fish, and any habitat of fish.

(10) The term "fishing" means:

(A) The catching, taking, or harvesting of fish;

(B) the attempted catching, taking or harvesting of fish;

(C) any other activity which can reasonably be expected to result in the catching, taking, or harvesting of fish; or

(D) any operations at sea in support of, or in preparation for, any activity described in subparagraphs (A) through (C).

Such term does not include any scientific research activity which is conducted by a scientific research vessel.

(11) The term "fishing vessel" means any vessel, boat, ship, or other craft which is used for, equipped to be used for, or of a type which is normally used for:

(A) fishing; or

(B) aiding or assisting one or more vessels at sea in the performance of any activity relating to fishing, including, but not limited to, preparation, supply, storage, refrigeration, transportation, or processing.

(12) The term "foreign fishing" means fishing by a vessel other than a vessel of the United States.

(13) The term "high seas" means all waters beyond the territorial sea of the United States and beyond any foreign nation's territorial sea, to the extent that such sea is recognized by the United States.

(14) The term "highly migratory species" means species of tuna which, in the course of their life cycle, spawn and migrate over great distances in waters of the ocean.

(15) The term "international fishery agreement" means any bilateral or multilateral treaty, convention, or agreement which relates to fishing and to which the United States is a party. . . .

(18) The term "optimum", with respect to the yield from a fishery, means the amount of fish:

(A) which will provide the greatest overall benefit to the Nation, with particular reference to food production and recreational opportunities; and

(B) which is prescribed as such on the basis of the maximum sustainable yield from such fishery, as modified by any relevant economic, social, or ecological factor.

(19) The term "person" means any individual (whether or not a citizen or national of the United States), any corporation, partnership, association, or other entity (whether or not organized or existing under the laws of any State), and any Federal, State, local, or foreign government or any entity of any such government.

(20) The term "Secretary" means the Secretary of Commerce or his designee.

(21) The term "State" means each of the several States, the District of Columbia, the Commonwealth of Puerto Rico, American Samoa, the Virgin Islands, Guam, and any other Commonwealth, territory, or possession of the United States.

(22) The term "stock of fish" means a species, subspecies, geographical grouping, or other category of fish capable of management as a unit.

(23) The term "treaty" means any international fishery agreement which

is a treaty within the meaning of section 2 of article II of the Constitution.

(24) The term "United States," when used in a geographical context, means all the States thereof.

(25) The term "vessel of the United States" means any vessel documented under the laws of the United States or registered under the laws of any State.

Title I. Fishery Management Authority of the United States

Sec. 101. Fishering Conservation Zone

There is established a zone contiguous to the territorial sea of the United States to be known as the fishery conservation zone. The inner boundary of the fishery conservation zone is a line coterminous with the seaward boundary of each of the coastal States, and the outer boundary of such zone is a line drawn in such a manner that each point on it is 200 nautical miles from the baseline from which the territorial sea is measured.

Sec. 102. Exclusive Fishery Management Authority

The United States shall exercise exclusive fishery management authority, in the manner provided for in this Act, over the following:

(1) All fish within the fishery conservation zone.

(2) All anadromous species throughout the migratory range of each such species beyond the fishery conservation zone; except that such management authority shall not extend to such species during the time they are found within any foreign nation's territorial sea or fishery conservation zone (or the equivalent), to the extent that such sea or zone is recognized by the United States.

(3) All Continental Shelf fishery resources beyond the fishery conservation zone.

Sec. 103. Highly Migratory Species

The exclusive fishery management authority of the United States shall not include, nor shall it be construed to extend to, highly migratory species of fish.

Sec. 104. Effective Date

This title shall take effect March 1, 1977.

Title II. Foreign Fishing and International Fishery Agreements

Sec. 201. Foreign Fishing

(a) *IN GENERAL.* After February 29, 1977, no foreign fishing is authorized within the fishery conservation zone, or for anadromous species or Continental Shelf fishery resources beyond the fishery conservation zone, unless such foreign fishing:

(1) is authorized under subsection (b) or (c);

(2) is not prohibited by subsection (f); and

(3) is conducted under, and in accordance with, a valid and applicable permit issued pursuant to section 204.

(b) *EXISTING INTERNATIONAL FISHERY AGREEMENTS.* Foreign fishing described in subsection (a) may be conducted pursuant to an international fishery agreement (subject to the provisions of section 202(b) or (c), if such agreement:

(1) was in effect on the data of enactment of this Act; and

(2) has not expired, been renegotiated, or otherwise ceased to be of force and effect with respect to the United States.

(c) *GOVERNING INTERNATIONAL FISHERY AGREEMENTS.* Foreign fishing described in subsection (a) may be conducted pursuant to an international fishery agreement (other than a treaty) which meets the requirements of this subsection if such agreement becomes effective after application of section 203. Any such international fishery agreement shall hereafter in this Act be referred to as a "governing international fishery agreement." Each governing international fishery agreement shall acknowledge the exclusive fishery management authority of the United States, as set forth in this Act. It is the sense of the Congress that each such agreement shall include a binding commitment, on the part of such foreign nation and its fishing vessels, to comply with the following terms and conditions:

(1) The foreign nation, and the owner or operator of any fishing vessel fishing pursuant to such agreement, will abide by all regulations promulgated by the Secretary pursuant to this Act, including any regulations promulgated to implement any applicable fishery management plan or any preliminary fishery management plan.

(2) The foreign nation, and the owner or operator of any fishing vessel fishing pursuant to such agreement, will abide by the requirement that:

(A) any officer authorized to enforce the provisions of this Act (as provided for in section 311) be permitted:

(i) to board, and search or inspect, any such vessel at any time,

(ii) to make arrests and seizures provided for in section 311(b) whenever such officer has reasonable cause to believe, as a result of such a search or inspection, that any such vessel or any person has committeed an act prohibited by section 307, and

(iii) to examine and make notations on the permit issued pursuant to section 204 for such vessel;

(B) the permit issued for any such vessel pursuant to section 204 be prominently displayed in the wheelhouse of such vessel;

(C) transponders, or such other appropriate positionfixing and identification equipment as the Secretary of the department in which the Coast Guard is operating determines to be appropriate, be installed and maintained in working order on each such vessel;

(D) duly authorized United States observers be permitted on board any such vessel and that the United States be reimbursed for the cost of such observers;

(E) any fees required under section 204(b) (10) be paid in advance;

(F) agents be appointed and maintained within the United States who are authorized to receive and respond to any legal process issued in the United States with respect to such owner or operator; and

(G) responsibility be assumed, in accordance with any requirements prescribed by the Secretary, for the reimbursement of United States citizens for any loss of, or damage to, their fishing vessels, fishing gear, or catch which is caused by any fishing vessel of that nation; and will abide by any other monitoring, compliance, or enforcement requirement related to fishery conservation and management which is included in such agreement.

(3) The foreign nation and the owners or operators of all of the fishing vessels of such nation shall not, in any year, exceed such nation's allocation of the total allowable level of foreign fishing, as determined under subsection (e).

(4) The foreign nation will:

(A) apply, pursuant to section 204, for any required permits;

(B) deliver promptly to the owner or operator of the appropriate fishing vessel any permit which is issued under that section for such vessel; and

(C) abide by, and take appropriate steps under its own laws to assure that all such owners and operators comply with, section 204(a) and the applicable conditions and restrictions established under section 204(b) (7).

(d) *TOTAL ALLOWABLE LEVEL OF FOREIGN FISHING.* The total allowable level of foreign fishing, if any, with respect to any fishery subject to the exclusive fishery management authority of the United States, shall be that portion of the optimum yield of such fishery which will not be harvested by vessels of the United States, as determined in accordance with the provisions of this Act.

(e) *ALLOCATION OF ALLOWABLE LEVEL.* The Secretary of State, in cooperation with the Secretary, shall determine the allocation among foreign nations of the total allowable level of foreign fishing which is permitted with respect to any fishery subject to the exclusive fishery management authority of the United States. In making any such determination, the Secretary of State and the Secretary shall consider:

(1) whether, and to what extent, the fishing vessels of such nations have traditionally engaged in fishing in such fishery;

(2) whether such nations have cooperated with the United States in, and made substantial contributions to, fishery research and the identification of fishery resources;

(3) whether such nationals have cooperated with the United States in enforcement and with respect to the conservation and management of fishery resources; and

(4) such other matters as the Secretary of State, in cooperation with the Secretary, deems appropriate.

(f) *RECIPROCITY.* Foreign fishing shall not be authorized for the fishing vessels of any foreign nation unless such nation satisfies the Secretary and the Secretary of State that such nation extends substantially the same fishing privileges to fishing vessels of the United States, if any, as the United States extends to foreign fishing vessels.

(g) *PRELIMINARY FISHERY MANAGEMENT PLANS.* The Secretary, when notified by the Secretary of State that any foreign nation has submitted an application under section 204(b), shall prepare a preliminary fishery management plan for any fishery covered by such application if the Secretary determines that no fishery management plan for that fishery will be prepared and implemented, pursuant to title III, before March 1, 1977. To the extent practicable, each such plan:

(1) shall contain a preliminary description of the fishery and a preliminary determination as to the optimum yield from such fishery and the total allowable level of foreign fishing with respect to such fishery;

(2) shall require each foreign fishing vessel engaged or wishing to engage in such fishery to obtain a permit from the Secretary;

(3) shall require the submission of pertinent data to the Secretary, with respect to such fishery, as described in section 303(a) (5); and

(4) may, to the extent necessary to prevent irreversible effects from overfishing, with respect to such fishery, contain conservation and management measures applicable to foreign fishing which:

(A) are determined to be necessary and appropriate for the conservation and management of such fishery,

(B) are consistent with the national standards, the other provisions of this Act, and other applicable law, and

(C) are described in section 303(b) (2), (3), (4), (5), and (7).

Each preliminary fishery management plan shall be in effect with respect to foreign fishing for which permits have been issued until a fishery management plan is prepared and implemented, pursuant to titale III, with respect to such fishery. The Secretary may, in accordance with section 553 of title 5, United States Code, also prepare and promulgate interim regulations with respect to any such preliminary plan. Such regulations shall be in effect until regulations implementing the applicable fishery management plan are promulgated pursuant to section 305.

Sec. 202. International Fishery Agreements

(a) *NEGOTIATIONS.* The Secretary of State:
(1) shall renegotiate treaties as provided for in subsection (b);
(2) shall negotiate governing international fishery agreements described in section 201(c);
(3) may negotiate boundary agreements as provided for in subsection (d);
(4) shall, upon the request of an in cooperation with the Secretary, initiate and conduct negotiations for the purpose of entering into international fishery agreements:
(A) which allow fishing vessels of the United States equitable access to fish over which foreign nations assert exclusive fishery management authority, and
(B) which provide for the conservation and management of anadromous species and highly migratory species; and
(5) may enter into such other negotiations, not prohibited by subsection (c), as may be necessary and appropriate to further the purposes, policy, and provisions of this Act.

(b) *TREATY RENEGOTIATION.* The Secretary of State, in cooperation with the Secretary, shall initiate, promptly after the date of enactment of this Act, the renegotiation of any treaty which pertains to fishing within the fishery conservation zone (or within the area that will constitute such zone after February 28, 1977), or for anadromous species or Continental Shelf fishery resources beyond such zone or area, and which is in any manner inconsistent with the purposes, policy, or provisions of this Act, in order to conform such treaty to such purposes, policy, and provisions. It is the sense of Congress that the United States shall withdraw from any such treaty, in accordance with its provisions, if such treaty is not so renegotiated within a reasonable period of time after such date of enactment.

(c) *INTERNATIONAL FISHERY AGREEMENTS.* No international fishery agreement (other than a treaty) which pertains to foreign fishing within the fishery conservation zone (or within the area that will constitute such zone after February 28, 1977), or for anadromous species or Continental Shelf fishery resources beyond such zone or area:

(1) which is in effect on June 1, 1976, may thereafter be renewed, extended, or amended; or

(2) may be entered into after May 31, 1976; by the United States unless it is in accordance with the provisions of section 201(c).

(d) *BOUNDARY NEGOTIATIONS.* The Secretary of State, in cooperation with the Secretary, may initiate and conduct negotiations with any adjacent or opposite foreign nation to establish the boundaries of the fishery conservation zone of the United States in relation to any such nation.

(e) *NONRECOGNITION.* It is the sense of the Congress that the United States Government shall not recognize the claim of any foreign nation to a fishery conservation zone (or the equivalent) beyond such nation's territorial sea, to the extent that such sea is recognized by the United States, if such nation:

(1) fails to consider and take into account traditional fishing activity of fishing vessels of the United States;

(2) fails to recognize and accept that highly migratory species are to be managed by applicable international fishery agreements, whether or not such nation is a party to any such agreement; or

(3) imposes on fishing vessels of the United States any conditions or restrictions which are unrelated to fishery conservation and management.

Sec. 203. Congressional Oversight of Governing International Fishery Agreements

(a) *IN GENERAL.* No governing international fishery agreement shall become effective with respect to the United States before the close of the first 60 calendar days of continuous session of the Congress after the date on which the President transmits to the House of Representatives and to the Senate a document setting forth the text of such governing international fishery agreement. A copy of the document shall be delivered to each House of Congress on the same day and shall be delivered to the Clerk of the House of Representatives, if the House is not in session, and to the Secretary of the Senate, if the Senate is not in session.

(b) *REFERRAL TO COMMITTEES.* Any document described in subsection (a) shall be immediately referred in the House of Representatives to the Committee on Merchant Marine and Fisheries, and in the Senate to the Committees on Commerce and Foreign Relations.

(c) *COMPUTATION OF 60-DAY PERIOD.* For purposes of subsection (a):

(1) continuity of session is broken only by an adjournment of Congress sine die; and

(2) the days on which either House is not in session because of an adjourn-ment of more than 3 days to a day certain are excluded in the computation of the 60-day period. . . .

Sec. 204. Permits for Foreign Fishing

(a) *IN GENERAL.* After February 28, 1977, no foreign fishing vessel shall engage in fishing within the fishery conservation zone, or for anadromous species or Continental Shelf fishery resources beyond such zone, unless such vessel has on board a valid permit issued under this section for such vessel.

(b) *APPLICATIONS AND PERMITS UNDER GOVERNING INTERNATION-AL FISHERY AGREEMENTS:*
    (1) *Eligibility.* Each foreign nation with which the United States has en-tered into a governing international fishery agreement shall submit an applica-tion to the Secretary of State each year for a permit for each of its fishing vessels that wishes to engage in fishing described in subsection (a).
    (2) *Forms.* The Secretary, in consultation with the Secretary of State and the Secretary of the department in which the Coast Guard is operating, shall prescribe the forms for permit applications submitted under this sub-section and for permits issued pursuant to any such application.
    (3) *Contents.* Any application made under this subsection shall specify:
    (A) the name and official number or other identification of each fishing vessel for which a permit is sought, together with the name and address of the owner therof;
    (B) the tonnage, capacity, speed, processing equipment, type and quanti-ty of fishing gear, and such other pertinent information with respect to char-acteristics of each such vessel as the Secretary may require;
    (C) each fishery in which each such vessel wishes to fish;
    (D) the amount of fish or tonnage of catch contemplated for each such vessel during the time such permit is in force; and
    (E) the ocean area in which, and the season or period during which, such fishing will be conducted; and shall include any other pertinent information and material which the Secretary may require.
    (4) *Transmittal for Action.* Upon receipt of any application which com-plies with the requirements of paragraph (3), the Secretary of State shall publish such application in the Federal Register and shall promptly transmit:
    (A) such application, together with his comments and recommendations thereon, to the Secretary;
    (B) a copy of the application to each appropriate Council and to the Secretary of the department in which the Coast Guard is operating; and
    (C) a copy of such material to the Committee on Merchant Marine and

Fisheries of the House of Representatives and to the Committees on Commerce and Foreign Relations of the Senate.

(5) *Action by Council.* After receipt of an application transmitted under paragraph (4) (B), each appropriate Council shall prepare and submit to the Secretary such written comments on the application as it deems appropriate. Such comments shall be submitted within 45 days after the date on which the application is received by the Council and may include recommendations with respect to approval of the application and, if approval is recommended, with respect to appropriate conditions and restrictions thereon. Any interested person may submit comments to such Council with respect to any such application. The Council shall consider any such comments in formulating its submission to the Secretary.

(6) *Approval.* After receipt of any application transmitted under paragraph (4) (A), the Secretary shall consult with the Secretary of State and, with respect to enforcement, with the Secretary of the department in which the Coast Guard is operating. The Secretary, after taking into consideration the views and recommendations of such Secretaries, and any comments submitted by any Council under paragraph (5), may approve the application, if he determines that the fishing described in the application will meet the requirements of this Act.

(7) *Establishment of Conditions and Restrictions.* The Secretary shall establish conditions and restrictions which shall be included in each permit issued pursuant to any application approved under paragraph (6) and which must be complied with by the owner or operator of the fishing vessel for which the permit is issued. Such conditions and restrictions shall include the following:

(A) All of the requirements of any applicable fishery management plan, or preliminary fishery management plan, and the regulations promulgated to implement any such plan.

(B) The requirement that no permit may be used by any vessel other than the fishing vessel for which it is issued.

(C) The requirements described in section 201(c) (1), (2), and (3).

(D) Any other condition and restriction related to fishery conservation and management which the Secretary prescribes as necessary and appropriate.

(8) *Notice of Approval.* The Secretary shall promptly transmit a copy of each application approved under paragraph (6) and the conditions and restrictions established under paragraph (7) to:

(A) the Secretary of State for transmittal to the foreign nation involved;

(B) the Secretary of the department in which the Coast Guard is operating;

(C) any Council which has authority over any fishery specified in such application; and

(D) the Committee on Merchant Marine and Fisheries of the House of

Representatives and the Committees on Commerce and Foreign Relations of the Senate.

(9) *Disapproval of Applications.* If the Secretary does not approve any application submitted by a foreign nation under this subsection, he shall promptly inform the Secretary of State of the disapproval and his reasons therefore. The Secretary of State shall notify such foreign nation of the disapproval and the reasons therefor. Such foreign nation, after taking into consideration the reasons for disapproval, may submit a revised application under this subsection.

(10) *Fees.* Reasonable fees shall be paid to the Secretary by the owner or operator of any foreign fishing vessel for which a permit is issued pursuant to this subsection. The Secretary, in consultation with the Secretary of State, shall establish and publish a schedule of such fees, which shall apply nondiscriminatorily to each foreign nation. In determining the level of such fees, the Secretary may take into account the cost of carrying out the provisions of this Act with respect to foreign fishing, including, but not limited to, the cost of fishery conservation and management, fisheries research, administration, and enforcement.

(11) *Issuance of Permits.* If a foreign nation notifies the Secretary of State of its acceptance of the conditions and restrictions established by the Secretary under paragraph (7), the Secretary of State shall promptly transmit such notification to the Secretary. Upon payment of the applicable fees established pursuant to paragraph (10), the Secretary shall thereupon issue to such foreign nation, through the Secretary of State, permits for the appropriate fishing vessels of that nation. Each permit shall contain a statement of all conditions and restrictions established under paragraph (7) which apply to the fishing vessel for which the permit is issued.

(12) *Sanctions.* If any foreign fishing vessel for which a permit has been issued pursuant to this subsection has been used in the commission of any act prohibited by section 307 the Secretary may, or if any civil penalty imposed under section 308 or any criminal fine imposed under section 309 has not been paid and is overdue the Secretary shall:

(A) revoke such permit, with or without prejudice to the right of the foreign nation involved to obtain a permit for such vessel in any subsequent year;

(B) suspend such permit for the period of time deemed appropriate; or

(C) impose additional conditions and restrictions on the approved application of the foreign nation involved and on any permit issued under such application.

Any permit which is suspended under this paragraph for nonpayment of a civil penalty shall be reinstated by the Secretary upon payment of such civil penalty together with interest theron at the prevailing rate.

(C) *Registration Permits.* The Secretary of State, in cooperation with the Secretary, shall issue annually a registration permit for each fishing vessel of a foreign nation which is a party to an international fishery agreement under which foreign fishing is authorized by section 201(b) and which wishes to engage in fishing described in subsection (a). Each such permit shall set forth the terms and conditions contained in the agreement that apply with respect to such fishing, and shall include the additional requirement that the owner or operator of the fishing vessel for which the permit is issued shall prominently display such permit in the wheelhouse of such vessel and show it, upon request, to any officer authorized to enforce the provisions of this Act (as provided for in section 311). The Secretary of State, after consultation with the Secretary and the Secretary of the department in which the Coast Guard is operating, shall prescribe the form and manner in which applications for registration permits may be made, and the forms of such permits. The Secretary of State may establish, require the payment of, and collect fees for registration permits; except that the level of such fees shall not exceed the administrative costs incurred by him in issuing such permits.

Sec. 205. Import Prohibitions

(a) *DETERMINATIONS BY SECRETARY OF STATE.* If the Secretary of State determines that:

(1) he has been unable, within a reasonable period of time, to conclude with any foreign nation an international fishery agreement allowing fishing vessels of the United States equitable access to fisheries over which that nation asserts exclusive fishery management authority, as recognized by the United States, in accordance with traditional fishing activities of such vessels, if any, and under terms not more restrictive than those established under sections 201(c) and (d) and 204(b) (7) and (10), because such nation has (A) refused to commence negotiations, or (B) failed to negotiate in good faith;

(2) any foreign nation is not allowing fishing vessels of the United States to engage in fishing for highly migratory species in accordance with an applicable international fishery agreement, whether or not such nation is a party thereto;

(3) any foreign nation is not complying with its obligations under any existing international fishery agreement concerning fishing by fishing vessels of the United States in any fishery over which that nation asserts exclusive fishery management authority; or

(4) any fishing vessel of the United States, while fishing in waters beyond any foreign nation's territorial sea, to the extent that such sea is recognized by the United States, is seized by any foreign nation:

(A) in violation of an applicable international fishery agreement;

(B) without authorization under an agreement between the United States and such nation; or

(C) as a consequence of a claim of jurisdiction which is not recognized by the United States; he shall certify such determination to the Secretary of the Treasury.

(b) *PROHIBITIONS.* Upon receipt of any certification from the Secretary of State under subsection (a), the Secretary of Treasury shall immediately take such action as may be necessary and appropriate to prohibit the importation into the United States:

(1) of all fish and fish products from the fishery involved, if any; and

(2) upon recommendation of the Secretary of State, such other fish or fish products, from any fishery of the foreign nation concerned, which the Secretary of State finds to be appropriate to carry out the purposes of this section.

(c) *REMOVAL OF PROHIBITION.* If the Secretary of State finds that the reasons for the imposition of any import prohibition under this section no longer prevail, the Secretary of State shall notify the Secretary of the Treasury, who shall promptly remove such import prohibition.

(d) *DEFINITIONS.* As used in this section:

(1) The term "fish" includes any highly migratory species.

(2) The term "fish products" means any article which is produced from or composed of (in whole or in part) any fish. . . .

Title III. National Fishery Management Program
[Sec. 301-306 omitted]

Sec. 307. Prohibited Acts

It is unlawful:

(1) for any person:

(A) to violate any provision of this Act or any regulation of permit issued pursuant to this Act;

(B) to use any fishing vessel to engage in fishing after the revocation, or during the period of suspension, of an applicable permit issued pursuant to this Act;

(C) to violate any provision of, or regulation under, an applicable governing international fishery agreement entered into pursuant to section 201(c);

(D) to refuse to permit any officer authorized to enforce the provisions of this Act (as provided for in section 311) to board a fishing vessel subject to such person's control for purposes of conducting any search or inspection in connection with the enforcement of this Act or any regulation, permit, or agreement referred to in subparagraph (A) or (C);

(E) to forcibly assault, resist, oppose, impeded, intimidate, or interfere with any such authorized officer in the conduct of any search or inspection described in subparagraph (D);

(F) to resist a lawful arrest for any act prohibited by this section;

(G) to ship, transport, offer for sale, sell, purchase, import, export, or have custody, control, or possession of, any fish taken or retained in violation of this Act or any regulation, permit, or agreement referred to in subparagraph (A) or (C); or

(H) to interfere with, delay, or prevent, by any means, the apprehension or arrest of another person, knowing that such other person has committed any act prohibited by this section; and

(2) for any vessel other than a vessel of the United States, and for the owner or operator of any vessel other than a vessel of the United States, to engage in fishing:

(A) within the boundaries of any State; or

(B) within the fishery conservation zone, or for any anadromous species or Continental Shelf fishery resources beyond such zone, unless such fishing is authorized by, and conducted in accordance with, a valid and applicable permit issued pursuant to section 204(b) or (c). . . .

(b) *POWERS OF AUTHORIZED OFFICERS.* Any officer who is authorized (by the Secretary, the Secretary of the department in which the Coast Guard is operating, or the head of any Federal or State agency which has entered into an agreement with such Secretaries under subsection (a)) to enforce the provisions of this Act may:

(1) with or without a warrant or other process:

(A) arrest any person, if he has reasonable cause to believe that such person has committed an act prohibited by section 307;

(B) board, and search or inspect, any fishing vessel which is subject to the provisions of this Act;

(C) seize any fishing vessel (together with its fishing gear, furniture, appurtenances, stores, and cargo) used or employed in, or with respect to which it reasonably appears that such vessel was used or employed in, the violation of any provision of this Act;

(D) seize any fish (wherever found) taken or retained in violation of any provision of this Act; and

(E) seize any other evidence related to any violation of any provision of this Act;

(2) execute any warrant or other process issued by any court of competent jurisdiction; and

(3) exercise any other lawful authority.

(c) *ISSUANCE OF CITATIONS.* If any officer authorized to enforce the provisions of this Act (as provided for in this section) finds that a fishing vessel is operating or has been operated in violation of any provision of this Act, such officer may, in accordance with regulations issued jointly by the Secretary and the Secretary of the Department in which the Coast Guard is operating, issue a citation to the owner or operator of such vessel in lieu of proceeding under subsection (b). If a permit has been issued pursuant to this Act for such vessel, such officer shall note the issuance of any citation under this subsection, including the date thereof and the reason therefor, on the permit. The Secretary shall maintain a record of all citations issued pursuant to this subsection.

(d) *JURISDICTION OF COURTS.* The district courts of the United States shall have exclusive jurisdiction over any case or controversy arising under the provisions of this Act. In the case of Guam, and any Commonwealth, territory, or possession of the United States in the Pacific Ocean, the appropriate court is the United States District Court for the District of Guam, except that in the case of American Samoa, the appropriate court is the United States District Court for the District of Hawaii. Any such court may, at any time:

(1) enter restraining orders or prohibitions;

(2) issue warrants, process in rem, or other process;

(3) prescribe and accept satisfactory bonds or other security; and

(4) take such other actions as are in the interest of justice.

(e) *DEFINITION.* For purposes of this section:

(1) The term "provisions of this Act" includes (A) any regulation or permit issued pursuant to this Act, and

(B) any provision of, or regulation issued pursuant to any international fishery agreement under which foreign fishing is authorized by section 201(b) or (c), with respect to fishing subject to the exclusive fishery management authority of the United States.

(2) The term "violation of any provision of this Act" includes (A) the commission of any act prohibited by section 307, and (B) the violation of any regulation, permit, or agreement referred to in paragraph (1).

Sec. 312. Effective Date of Certain Provisions

Sections 307, 308, 309, 310, and 311 shall take effect March 1, 1977.

Title IV. Miscellaneous Provisions

Sec. 401. Effect on Law of the Sea Treaty

If the United State ratifies a comprehensive treaty, which includes provisions with respect to fishery conservation and management jurisdiction, resulting from any United Nations Conference on the Law of the Sea, the Secretary, after consultation with the Secretary of State, may promulgate any amendment to the regulations promulgated under this Act if such amendment is necessary and appropriate to conform such regulations to the provisions of such treaty, in anticipation of the date when such treaty shall come into force and effect for, or otherwise be applicable to, the United States. . . .

Bibliography

Books

Burke, William T., et al., National and International Law Enforcement in the Ocean. Seattle, Wash.: University of Washington Press, 1975.

Christy, Francis T., Jr., Alternative Arrangements for Marine Fisheries: An Overview. Washington, D.C.: Resources for the Future, Inc., 1973.

_____, and Anthony Scott, The Common Wealth in Ocean Fisheries. Baltimore, Md.: Johns Hopkins Press, 1965.

Crutchfield, James, The Fisheries: Problems in Resource Management. Seattle, Wash.: University of Washington Press, 1965.

_____, and Rowena Lawson, West African Marine Fisheries: Alternatives for Management. Washington, D.C.: Resources for the Future, Inc., 1974.

_____, and Giulio Pontecorvo, The Pacific Salmon Fisheries: A Study of Irrational Conservation. Washington, D.C.: Resources for the Future, Inc., 1969.

Cushing, David, Fisheries Resources of the Sea and Their Management. London: Oxford University Press, 1975.

Fenn, Percy Thomas, Jr., The Origin of the Right of Fishery in Territorial Waters. Cambridge, Mass.: Harvard University Press, 1926.

Gilbert, D., ed., The Future of the Fishing Industry of the United States. Seattle, Wash.: University of Washington Press, 1968.

Gulland, J.A., The Management of Marine Fisheries. Seattle, Wash.: University of Washington Press, 1974.

Hjertonsson, Karin, The New Law of the Sea: Influence of the Latin American States on Recent Developments of the Law of the Sea. Leiden, The Netherlands: A.W. Sijthoff, 1973.

Jessup, Philip C., The Law of Territorial Waters and Maritime Jurisdiction. New York: G.A. Jennings Co., Inc., 1927.

Johnston, Douglas M., The International Law of Fisheries. New Haven, Conn.: Yale University Press, 1965.

Kasahara, Hiroshi, and William T. Burke, North Pacific Fisheries Management. Washington, D.C.: Resources for the Future, Inc., 1973.

Knight, H. Gary, ed., The Future of International Fisheries Management. St. Paul, Minn.: West Publishing Company (Washington, D.C.: © American Society of International Law), 1975.

Koers, Albert W., International Regulation of Marine Fisheries. London: Fishing News (Books) Ltd., 1973.

Leonard, L. Larry, International Regulation of Fisheries. Washington, D.C.: Carnegie Endowment for International Peace, 1944.

131

McDougal, Myres S., and William T. Burke, The Public Order of the Ocean. New Haven, Conn.: Yale University Press, 1962.

Miles, Edward, Organizational Arrangements to Facilitate Global Management of Fisheries. Washington, D.C.: Resources for the Future, Inc., 1974.

Oda, Shigeru, International Control of Sea Resources. Leiden, The Netherlands: A.W. Sijthoff, 1963.

Osgood, Robert E., et al., Toward a National Ocean Policy: 1976 and Beyond. Washington, D.C.: U.S. Government Printing Office, 1976.

Pontecorvo, Giulio, ed., Fisheries Conflicts in the North Atlantic: Problems of Management and Jurisdiction. Cambridge, Mass.: Ballinger Publishing Company, 1974.

Roedel, Philip M., ed., Optimum Sustainable Yield as a Concept in Fisheries Management. Washington, D.C.: American Fisheries Society, 1975.

Rothschild, Brian J., ed., World Fisheries Policy: Multidisciplinary Views. Seattle, Wash.: University of Washington Press, 1972.

Saila, Saul B., and Virgil J. Norton, Tuna: Status, Trends, and Alternative Management Arrangements. Washington, D.C.: Resources for the Future, Inc., 1974.

Sainsbury, John C., Commercial Fishing Methods: An Introduction to Vessels and Gear. London: Fishing News (Books) Ltd., 1971.

Scott, A.D., ed., Economics of Fisheries Management: A Symposium. Vancouver, B.C.: University of British Columbia, 1970.

Tussing, Arlon R., and Robin A. Hiebert, Fisheries of the Indian Ocean: Issues of International Management and Law of the Sea. Washington, D.C.: Resources for the Future, Inc., 1974.

Articles

Allen, Edward W., "International Law, War, and Fish," *Tulane Law Review* 18 (1943): 118.

Alverson, Dayton L., "Opportunities to Increase Food Production from the World's Ocean," *M.T.S. Journal* 9 (1975), no. 5): 33.

Anderson, Hans G., "The Icelandic Fishery Limits and the Concept of the Exclusive Economic Zone," *Ulfljotur* 27 (1974 Supp., no. 3): 3.

Anderson, Lee G., "Economic Aspects of Fisheries Utilization in the Law of the Sea Negotiations," *San Diego Law Review* 11 (1974): 656.

——— , "Optimum Economic Yield of a Fishery Given a Variable Price of Output," *Journal of the Fisheries Resources Board of Canada* 30 (1973): 509.

Azzam, Issum,"Dispute between France and Brazil over Lobster Fishing in the Atlantic," *The International and Comparative Law Quarterly* 13 (1964): 1453.

Bilder, Richard, "The Anglo-Icelandic Fisheries Dispute," *Wisconsin Law Review* 1973 (1973): 37.

Bromley, Daniel, and Victor Arnold, "Social Goals, Problem Perception, and Public Intervention: The Fishery," *San Diego Law Review* 7 (1970): 469.

Burke, William T., "Some Thoughts on Fisheries and a New Conference on the Law of the Sea," Occasional Paper no. 9, Law of the Sea Institute, University of Rhode Island (1971).

Carroz, J.E., and A.G. Roche, "The International Policing of High Seas Fisheries," *Canadian Year Book of International Law* 6 (1968): 61.

Chapman, Wilbert M., "The Theory and Practice of International Fishery Development-Management," *San Diego Law Review* 7 (1970): 408.

Christy, Francis T., "Fisheries and the New Conventions on the Law of the Sea," *San Diego Law Review* 7 (1970): 455.

Churchill, Robin, "The Fisheries Jurisdiction Cases: The Contribution of the International Court of Justice to the Debate on Coastal States' Fisheries Rights," *The International and Comparative Law Quarterly* 24 (1975): 82.

Crutchfield, James A., "Economic and Political Objectives in Fishery Management," *Transactions of the American Fisheries Society* 102 (1973): 481.

Edeson, William, "The Impact on Fisheries of Two-Hundred Mile Zones," *Maritime Studies and Management* 2 (1975): 138.

Eisenbud, Robert, "Understanding the International Fisheries Debate," Natural *Resources Lawyer* 4 (1971): 19.

Fidell, Eugene R., "Hot Pursuit from a Fisheries Zone," *American Journal of International Law* 70 (1976): 95.

———, "Ten Years under the Bartlett Act: A Status Report on the Prohibition on Foreign Fishing," *Boston University Law Review* 54 (1974): 703.

Finkle, Peter, "The International Commission for the Northwest Atlantic Fisheries: An Experiment in Conservation," *Dalhousie Law Journal* 1 (1974): 526.

Food and Agriculture Organization, "Report on Regulatory Fishery Bodies," Food and Agriculture Organization Fisheries Circular No. 138 (1972).

Goldie, L.F.E., "The Oceans' Resources and International Law—Possible Developments in Regional Fisheries Management," *Columbia Journal of Transnational Law* 8 (1969): 1.

Hayashi, Moritaka, "Soviet Policy on International Regulation of High Seas Fisheries," *Cornell International Law Journal* 5 (1972): 131.

Jacobs, Michael J., "United States Participation in International Fisheries Agreements," *Journal of Maritime Law and Commerce* 6 (1975): 471.

Jacobson, Jon L., "Future Fishing Technology and its Impact on the Law of the Sea," in Francis T. Christy, et al., eds., *The Law of the Sea: Caracas and Beyond.* Cambridge, Mass.: Ballinger, 1975, at 237.

———., "Bridging the Gap to International Fisheries Agreement: A Guide for Unilateral Action," *San Diego Law Review* 9 (1972): 454.

Johnson, Barbara, "A Review of Fisheries Proposals Made at the Caracas Session of LOS III," *Ocean Management* 2 (1975): 285.

———, "Technocrats and the Management of International Fisheries," *International Organization* 29 (1975): 745.

Kahn, Rahmatullah, "The Fisheries Jurisdiction Case—A Critique," *Indian Journal of International Law* 15 (1975): 1.

———, "On the Fairer and Equitable Sharing of the Fishery Resources of the Oceans," *Indian Journal of International Law* 13 (1973): 87.

Kask, J., "Tuna—A World Resource," Occasional Paper no. 2, Law of the Sea Institute, University of Rhode Island (1969).

Knight, H. Gary, "International Fisheries Management without Global Agreement: United States Policies and their Impact on the Soviet Union," *Georgia Journal of International and Comparative Law* 6 (1976): 119.

Koers, Albert W., "Fishery Proposals in the United Nations Seabed Committee: An Evaluation," *Journal of Maritime Law and Commerce* 5 (1974): 183.

———, "The International Regulation of Marine Fisheries: Some Problems and Proposals," *Annals of International Studies* 4 (1973): 191.

———, "The Enforcement of International Fisheries Agreements," *Netherlands Year Book of International Law* 1 (1970): 1.

Kury, Channing, "The Fisheries Proposals: An Assessment," *San Diego Law Review* 12 (1975): 644.

Lakshmanan, R., "International Regulation of Fisheries," *Indian Journal of International Law* 13 (1973): 367.

Liston, John, and Lynwood Smith, "Fishing and the Fishing Industry: An Account with Comments on Overseas Technology Transfer," *Ocean Development and International Law Journal* 2 (1974): 285 and 2 (1975): 313.

Meron, Theodor, "The Fishermen's Protective Act: A Case Study in Contemporary Legal Strategy of the United States," *American Journal of International Law* 69 (1975): 290.

Moiseev, P.A., "Some Biological Background for International Legal Acts on Rational Utilization of the Living Resources of the World Ocean," *Georgia Journal of International and Comparative Law* 6 (1976): 143.

Oda, Shigeru, "New Directions in the International Law of Fisheries," *Japanese Annals of International Law* 17 (1973): 84.

———, "Distribution of Fish Resources of the High Sea: Free Competition or Artificial Quota?" in Lewis M. Alexander, ed., *The Law of the Sea: The Future of the Sea's Resources*. Kingston, R.I.: University of Rhode Island, 1968, at 29.

Ottenheimer, Gerald R., "Patterns of Development in International Fishery Law," *Canadian Year Book of International Law* 11 (1973): 37.

Robison, John T., "Ocean Fisheries: National Instrument for International Stability," *Naval War College Review* 21 (1969, no. 10): 106.

Schaefer, Milner B., "Some Recent Developments Concerning Fishing and the Conservation of the Living Resources of the High Seas," *San Diego Law Review* 7 (1970): 371.

Shyam, M., "Rights of the Coastal States to Fisheries Resources in the Economic Zone: An Empirical Analysis of State Preferences," *Ocean Management* 3 (1976, no. 1): 1.

Snow, Steven E., "The Establishment of International Fisheries Claims Boards for the Resolution of Fishery-Related Disputes: Their Implementation, Procedures, and Effectiveness," *American University Law Review* 24 (1975): 1333.

Taft, George, "The Third U.N. Law of the Sea Conference: Major Unresolved Fisheries Issues," *Columbia Journal of Transnational Law* 14 (1975): 112.

Van der Mensbrugghe, Y., "The Common Market Fisheries Policy and the Law of the Sea," *Netherlands Year Book of International Law* 6 (1975): 199.

Walker, Richard K., and James L. McNish, "Toward a Model Regional Fisheries Management Regime: An Immodest Proposal," *Kansas Law Review* 23 (1975): 461.

Windley, David W., "International Practice Regarding Traditional Fishing Privileges of Foreign Fishermen in Zones of Extended Maritime Jurisdiction," *American Journal of International Law* 63 (1969): 490.

Wolff, Thomas, "Peruvian-United States Relations over Maritime Fishing: 1945-1969," Occasional Paper no. 4, Law of the Sea Institute, University of Rhode Island (1970).

Index

abstention doctrine, 43

allocation of fishery resources, 41–45; abstention, 43; administration, 44; bilateral agreements, 42; distant water fishing, 41; equity, 37; historic rights, 41–42; landlocked states, 44–45; open access, 43–44

anadromous species, definition, 10; proposals in law of the sea conference, 62–63; Revised Single Negotiating Text, 65, 108–109; US industry, 77

Atlantic Ocean, 13, 51

Bartlett Act, 76, 78; repeal, 88

baseline, 19–21, 25

bilateral fishery agreements, 42

biology. *See* fisheries, biology

Brazil, 36, 51–52; shrimp agreement with US, 70

Canada, bar of Soviet vessels, 71; proposal on anadromous species, 62–63; 200-mile fisheries zone claim, 69

Chile. *See* "tuna war"

closed seas, 13, 15–16

coastal species, definition, 9; Revised Single Negotiating Text, 64–65, 107–108; US industry, 77

"cod war," 1, 36, 51, 72, 80; decision of International Court of Justice, 66–69

commissions, effect of 200-mile fishing zone zones, 73; natures and functions, 47–48

conflict avoidance, 36–37

conservation, 38–41; administration, 39–40; costs of, 41; enforcement, 40; maximum sustainable yield

(*see* maximum sustainable yield); Revised Single Negotiating Text, 105–107

contiguous zone, 21–22, 26

continental shelf, apportionment among adjacent states, 25; Convention on, 22, 25, 28, 36, 76; customary international law, 81; definition and concept, 22, 25; seaward limit, 22; sedentary species of (*see* sedentary species)

Convention on Fishing and Conservation of the Living Resources of the High Seas, 26, 34, 75

Convention on the Continental Shelf. *See* continental shelf, Convention on

Convention on the High Seas. *See* high seas, Convention on

Convention on the Territorial Sea and the Contiguous Zone. *See* territorial sea, Convention on

Convention on Transit Trade of Landlocked Countries, 44

creeping jurisdiction, 66

customary international law, 17, 81

Declaration of Santo Domingo, 60

Denmark, anadromous species proposal, 63

distant water fishing nations' proposals, 59–60

economics. *See* fisheries, economics

Ecuador. *See* "tuna war"

enforcement, 40, 48, 87; under Fishery Conservation and Management Act of 1976, 127–129

England, 13, 16, 36, 51; "cod war" decision of International Court of Justice, 66–69

About the Author

H. Gary Knight is a graduate of Stanford University and the Southern Methodist University School of Law. He practiced law in Los Angeles, California, from 1964 to 1968 before joining the faculty of the Louisiana State University Law Center where he is now Campanile Professor of Marine Resources Law. He has been involved in the current law of the sea negotiations since their inception at the United Nations in 1967, and has served since 1972 as a member of the Advisory Committee on the Law of the Sea (National Security Council Inter-Agency Law of the Sea Task Force). He has written widely on law of the sea issues and specifically on international fishery management problems, including two studies for the National Marine Fisheries Service. Professor Knight is an associate editor of *Ocean Development and International Law: A Journal of Marine Affairs,* and serves on the Executive Board of the Law of the Sea Institute. He was a consultant to the Office of the Law of the Sea, U.S. Department of State, in 1974–75, is a member of the Board of Review and Development of the American Society of International Law, and is a member of the American branch of the International Law Association.